FROGS & TOADS
OF THE
WORLD

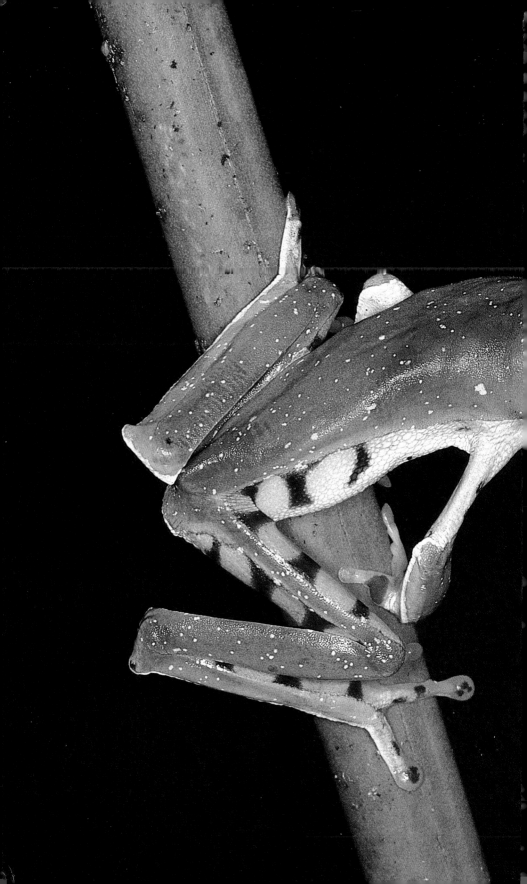

FROGS & TOADS
OF THE
WORLD

Chris Mattison

BLANDFORD

Frogs & Toads of the World

Paperback edition first published in the UK 1992
by Blandford, a Cassell imprint

Cassell plc
Wellington House
125 Strand
London WC2R 0BB

Reprinted 1998 & 1999
Previously published in hardback by Blandford in 1987
Reprinted 1989 & 1994 (USA)

Distributed in the United States by Sterling Publishing Co., Inc.,
387 Park Avenue South, New York, NY 10016–8810

**A Cataloguing-in-Publication Data entry for this title
is available from the British Library**

ISBN 0-7137-2355-6

Typeset by Graficraft Typesetters Ltd, Hong Kong
Printed in Hong Kong by Colorcraft Ltd

Contents

Acknowledgements

Before singling out those persons who, through their direct help, deserve special mention, it is important that I thank all the numerous friends and colleagues who have helped and encouraged me throughout this book's early development and eventual metamorphosis: I can only hope that those who remain anonymous will nevertheless realise that their efforts are greatly appreciated.

Possibly my greatest fortune has been the good company I have enjoyed during field trips. In this way Robin Mattison, Bill Montgomery (twice), Isabelle Naylor and Dave Resnick have contributed, not only in practical ways but, more importantly, by retaining their good humour and patience under conditions which were often uncomfortable and sometimes downright unhealthy!

In addition, Bill Montgomery collected several specimens for me in Texas, while the following people allowed me to photograph animals in their care: John Pickett, James Savage, Peter van Leeuwen, Paul Walker and Xotic Pets of Alfreton. The specimen in plate 16 was expertly prepared and photographed by Roger Webb and David Hollingworth respectively, and Professor Charles Myers (American Museum of Natural History), John Simmons (Kansas University) and Dr Mike Tyler (University of Adelaide) kindly took time out from their own research to respond to my requests for information. I am especially indebted to Isabelle Naylor, whose skilfully prepared line drawings enhance the following pages, and who also made a number of helpful suggestions regarding the text. Finally, thanks to the editors of Blandford Press who, once again, awaited the manuscript with great patience.

Introduction

This book of about 50,000 words deals with a group of animals of which there are 3,500 species: an average of just over fourteen words per species. It must therefore be a book of generalities rather than a thorough systematic account. However, in researching it, both in the library and in the field, certain aspects of frog biology and certain groups of species have captured my imagination more than others and it is inevitable that these subjects are covered in greatest detail: I can only hope that they appeal equally to the reader.

Frogs and toads are fascinating animals: to the layman, their bulging eyes and hopping gait are the stuff of fairy tales and superstitions; to the biologist, recent observations on their social behaviour have led to an upsurge in interest which will, I predict, continue to grow until they vie with other groups of animals for serious attention by behavioural ecologists. Furthermore, their dependence on two environments at different stages in their lives effectively doubles the scope for investigation.

And lastly, they live in such wonderful places: swamps and rivers, deserts and mountains and, especially, in tropical forests – the richest (and most vulnerable) habitat on earth, where the evolution of frogs seems to have run riot. Although it is not possible adequately to describe the feelings of a naturalist visiting one of these places for the first time, I can think of no better way to introduce the world of frogs and toads than to guide the reader along a short walk through a tropical forest.

The location is South East Asia, but it could just as well be South America, Africa or Australia – only the individual species vary.

Shod in a pair of old canvas sneakers and armed with a stick or metal hook (for flipping over dead leaves), a waterproof torch and, most importantly, plenty of mosquito repellent, we set off just before dusk, as the last few drops of a heavy tropical downpour are wrung from the clouds.

As we enter the forest, our eyes take some time to adjust to the shade, but a movement at our feet gives away a young toad, *Bufo asper*, hopping purposefully across our path. A promising start, even though this is one of the commonest forest species, and we press on, guided by the roar of the river nearby – just a trickle this morning but now swollen by the heavy rains in the mountains nearby. Before reaching it our path skirts an open marshy area which marks the transition between land and water. Even away from the trees, the light is falling now and the first tentative sounds of what will become a full symphony of frog choruses can be heard – the orchestra is tuning up. Using the torches for the first time, we begin to track down the source of these calls. It takes a little time to find the first one, a pale brown tree frog, *Polypedates leucomystax*, calling from a low shrub at the edge of the marsh, but once he has been located others are found more easily, all in similar positions – they are intent on attracting females, but only a few will be successful tonight.

In the meantime, the raucous squawking of *Polypedates* has been joined by two other tunes, a much repeated croak and a more refined chirping. The sounds are all around us now and as we arrive at a small body of open water the 'croakers' reveal themselves: green and bronze striped *Rana erythraea*, calling from shallow water, and making off with great leaps as we splash towards them. The 'chirpers' take a little longer to spot – they are calling from small tufts of grass growing in a millimetre or two of water. It is difficult to home in on the short calls and they stop completely every time we approach, only to be replaced by similar calls to one side or the other. We zig-zag from source to source becoming more and more frustrated, but by painstakingly parting the individual blades of grass where we were certain (almost) that a call was heard a few minutes ago, a tiny frog is discovered. It turns out to be *Microhyla butleri*, a putty-coloured species with darker blotches on its back, a member of a large but inconspicuous family of ground-dwelling and burrowing frogs found in many parts of the world. By the time the possibilities of the marsh are exhausted it is totally dark and, as we reach the river bank, the torches pick out pale shapes clinging to the partly submerged rocks. These are torrent frogs, *Amolops larutensis*, superbly equipped for the environment in which they live by means of large discs at the tips of all their digits which enable them to adhere to the wet and slippery surfaces. We get too close to one and it leaps backwards into the swirling water, its arms and legs flaying, only to reappear a few inches away. Lower down on the rocks are their even more remarkable tadpoles, attached like tailed limpets with their sucker-like mouths. Every few seconds they are lost from view as the water gushes over them but are soon exposed again, glistening, as it recedes. In this way they exploit the layer of bacterial and algal slime which grows best on this zone of the rock, and they wriggle from place to place, never releasing their grip or they will be swept away. We continue down-river, finding more *Amolops* – juveniles, sub-adults and adults – on almost every mid-stream rock, until we reach a place where the river is joined by a small stream flowing down over rocks and tree-roots, so forming a series of small pools.

Following this corridor up through the forest, the roar of the main river is muted and a new call, a strange explosive metallic 'Ching!' can be heard. This time we know which animal produces the sound – a horned toad, *Megophrys nasuta*, one of the most bizarre forest animals, beautifully camouflaged in colour and shape to blend into the carpet of leaves which covers the ground. This makes it a difficult animal to find, as we know from previous fruitless searches, but tonight it is calling more vigorously than ever, stimulated by the recent rains. Even so, they call only sporadically, a single note, and stop completely at the least disturbance. Nor do they form a chorus, just three or four males, spaced out along the

stream, the calls of the furthest ones barely audible. Great patience is required now. Each time the nearest toad calls we move a few yards towards it, slowly working our way up the stream – but then the calling stops. Have we frightened it away, or is courtship over for the evening? Resisting the temptation to start searching haphazardly, we crouch in the water, torches off, and wait. For ten minutes the darkness is relieved only by the faint glow of small luminescent fungi growing on the dead leaves and twigs along the stream. Just as we begin to think that the toad is gone, the 'ching!' sounds again, startling us with its closeness, and we switch on the torches, directing the beams at a raised section of the bank from which the sound seemed to originate. Leaves are examined closely, our imagination turning each one into a toad, until a *Megophrys* suddenly materialises, the front of its body raised slightly, its throat still partially inflated in readiness to call again. Its black eyes stare inscrutably into the light but it remains motionless, relying entirely on its near-perfect camouflage. How many of these have we walked past on previous nights? Where do they go during the day, and where are their mates?

This account is not fanciful: frog-hunting in the tropics can, apart from satisfying the hunting instinct which is in all of us, provide an insight into the varied lives of an interesting group of animals, produce the answers to some of our questions but, at the same time, raise others – and this is exactly what this book aims to do.

Chapter 1
Frogs or Toads?

Frogs and toads belong to the order Anura, the tailless amphibians, consisting of about 3,500 members. Along with three other smaller orders, the caecilians (Apoda), containing about 150 species, the sirens (Trachystomata), containing just three species and the salamanders (Caudata), containing about 350 species, they form the important class Amphibia, or amphibians. The early amphibians were the first vertebrates to give up an aquatic existence and begin the colonisation of the land, about 350 million years ago (although the frogs and toads, oldest of the surviving orders, didn't appear for another 200 million years). They still retain a close affinity with water, having glandular skins which must be kept moist, and most species return to water to lay eggs. These develop into aquatic gill-breathing larvae (tadpoles) before undergoing metamorphosis to the terrestrial stage of their lives. (The word 'amphibian' is derived from two Greek words, *amphi* = both, and *bios* = life.) A number of species, including some of the frogs and toads, are totally aquatic, although they still breathe by means of lungs and must therefore come to the surface from time to time. Other species have become arboreal, rarely if ever coming down to ground level, and several spend their entire lives in underground burrows or chambers. Somewhere along their evolutionary path the frogs and toads acquired voices – a variety of croaks, trills, grunts and whistles, each unique to a particular species and therefore of great value in defining territories, attracting mates and recognising other individuals of their kind.

What is the difference between frogs and toads? This is one of the most frequently asked questions when these animals are under discussion, and one of the most difficult to explain. To find the answer it is necessary to remember that when these two words were coined, only two sorts of anurans were recognised: *the* frog, later to be known as *Rana temporaria*, a moist and slimy creature which jumps, and *the* toad, *Bufo bufo*, which is dry and warty and walks. As new species came to be found in other regions, the two vernacular names were applied to them according to their superficial resemblance to one or the other of the 'models'. Unfortunately, things are rarely so simple in nature, and confusion arises over families which contain both moist slimy species as well as dry warty ones. It may be less confusing if we think of all the tailless amphibia as frogs, and use the word toad in its narrower sense, i.e. for members of the family Bufonidae, but throughout this and other books various departures from this rule will be noticed, for example, *Alytes obstetricans*, the midwife 'toad', belongs to the same family as *Discoglossus pictus*, the

Plate 2   *Rana temporaria*, the common frog of Europe.

Plate 3   *Bufo bufo*, the common toad of Europe. These two species inadvertently started the confusion over the terms 'frog' and 'toad'.

painted 'frog', and so on – the labels applied by the early zoologists have become so firmly fixed in our memories that it would be foolish and even more confusing to try to rationalise them.

Over the years, scientists have sorted and re-sorted the known species of frogs and toads into groups which have evolved from a common ancestor and are therefore closely related. Confusion has often arisen over species which have evolved independently but are superficially similar due to similar environmental pressures (parallel, or convergent, evolution) and it is often necessary to look closely at some seemingly obscure anatomical feature before an accurate assessment can be made of the relationships between one group of species and another. In many cases, intermediate forms have become extinct and so there are large gaps in the transitional series from one kind to another.

As the methods for classifying animals become more and more sophisticated with the use of modern techniques such as electrophoresis and computer analysis, the inadequacies and inaccuracies of previous systems of classification become apparent, leading to constant revisions within the order. Superimposed on this situation are the differing opinions of experts as to the relationships between certain species, genera and families. This is often confusing, not to say irritating, to the naturalist, who would obviously prefer to see a more stable situation, but it should be realised that these names which we give to animals are only labels, applied for our own convenience, and they should not become an obsession in themselves.

Apart from those species which hail from Europe and North America (a relatively tiny proportion of the total), frogs and toads are rarely blessed with widely accepted common names. It is usually necessary, therefore, to use latinised names, each consisting of two or three units: the genus, species and sub-species respectively, as follows: *Hyla arborea japonica*, where *Hyla* is the genus (tree-frogs); *arborea* is the species (a wide-ranging Eurasian tree-frog); and *japonica* is the sub-species (the form which is found in Japan). Only the genus begins with a capital letter, but the whole of the name is printed in italics. Where no sub-species are recognised, or where a passage refers to all of the sub-species of the species concerned, then only the first two names are necessary, e.g. *Hyla arborea*.

Throughout this book I have followed a fairly conservative system of classification, based on that of Duellman and Trueb (see references), in which twenty-one families of frogs are recognised, whereas others have proposed up to thirty families, the distinction between some of which is minimal and controversial.

Many of these families may be further divided into sub-families, although I feel that there is insufficient information regarding the origins and evolution of frogs to describe these with any degree of conviction. I have therefore taken the easy way out, and referred to sub-families only at odd places through the text where these are reasonably well defined and form a useful means of grouping together species which have obvious close affinities and share the characteristics under discussion.

13

Table 1: The families of frogs and toads

Leiopelmatidae (tailed frog, New Zealand frogs)	4
Discoglossidae (painted frogs, fire-bellied toads, midwife toads)	14
Rhinophrynidae (Mexican burrowing frog)	1
Pipidae (clawed frogs, Surinam toads, etc.)	26
Pelobatidae (spadefoot toads, etc.)	83
Pelodytidae (parsley frogs)	2
Myobatrachidae	106
Heleophrynidae (ghost frogs)	3
Sooglossidae	3
Leptodactylidae	710
Bufonidae (toads)	335
Brachycephalidae (short-headed toads)	2
Rhinodermatidae	2
Pseudidae	4
Hylidae (tree frogs)	630
Centrolenidae	65
Dendrobatidae (poison dart frogs)	117
Ranidae	667
Hyperoliidae (reed frogs, etc.)	206
Rhacophoridae	186
Microhylidae	279

Total: 3445 species in 310 genera and 21 families

Identification

The first step towards studying frogs and toads at any level is the ability to distinguish one species from the rest and put a name to it. Naturalists living in Europe, North America, South Africa and Australia are fortunate in having excellent field guides (see Bibliography) which will enable them to do just this. In other parts of the world, however, the situation is not nearly so easy, either because the frog fauna is not well enough known, or because there is insufficient local interest (often both). In order to identify species from these places, a certain amount of detective work will be necessary, along with the ability to use a scientific key (if there is one for the area). These make use of characteristics such as pupil shape, the amount of webbing between the digits, the presence or absence of enlarged glands, toe-pads or a visible tympanum, etc., to 'key out' specimens. Unfortunately, most scientific keys are based on museum specimens in which the colour has faded and so this may not be included in the key, and nor will aspects of behaviour. Figure 1 is a diagrammatic frog showing the location of some of the more obvious features which are often used in this type of key, and a number of keys for various parts of the world are listed in the Bibliography.

Identification of tadpoles is notoriously difficult. Four morphological

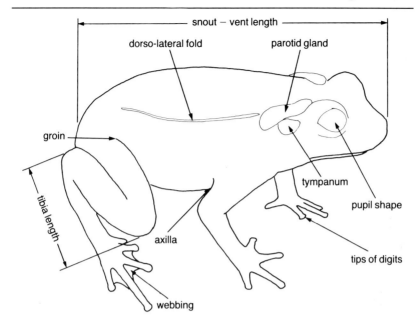

Fig. 1   The main external diagnostic features of a frog.

types are easily recognisable (fig. 15, page 101), which correspond to families, but Type IV tadpoles are by far the commonest and are associated with over 90 per cent of the known species. Although keys to tadpoles exist, for the most part it is only possible to recognise a few of the more distinctive species and, if identification is important, it may be necessary to rear some to metamorphosis and beyond in order to achieve this.

The origin of frogs and toads

If our knowledge of the living frogs and toads seems patchy, our knowledge of their ancestors is almost non-existent. Almost every expert who has looked into the subject has arrived at a different theory and there is not room here for a full discussion – Chapter 15 of Duellman and Trueb's *Biology of Amphibians* reviews the current opinions and the interested reader is referred to that account. Therefore, only a brief survey is attempted here.

It is widely believed that the amphibians evolved from a group of fishes known as the lobe-fins (crossopterygians), which lived during the Devonian period, 350–400 million years ago. An alternative theory is that they arose from the lung-fish (Dipnoi), the remaining five species of which still survive in parts of South America, Africa and Australia. Whichever is the case, the earliest amphibians almost certainly evolved in shallow fresh-water lakes, possibly as a result of these drying out during periods of warm climate. (Some modern lung-fish face the same problem and overcome it by burrowing into the mud and forming a cocoon around themselves.) Their new way of life required a number of important modifications, amongst which were a more freely articulating skeleton, allowing movement of the head and limbs in relation to the backbone, development of glands which would keep the skin moist, and an eye which was effective in their new medium, air. They were carnivorous and may have fed on fish which were trapped in the drying lakes and pools, and on each other.

Fossils of the oldest amphibian come from Greenland, and were formed at the end of the Devonian period, about 350 million years ago. Three species have been recognised, of which the best preserved material comes from an animal known as *Ichthyostega*, which has a tail with a long dorsal fin, many teeth and a short blunt snout. It measured about one metre in total length.

One hundred million years later, during the Permian period, *Ichthyostega* and its close relatives appear to have died out, having given rise to three distinct sub-classes of amphibians: the Labrythodontia, which were the ancestors of the reptiles; the Leptospondyli, which appears to have been a dead end in evolutionary terms; and a third group, the Lissamphibia, which contains all the surviving amphibians. Unfortunately, all of the early Lissamphibia are unknown as fossils and so it is a matter of conjecture as to whether the salamanders, caecilians and frogs arose from a common stem or independently (many authorities believe that the salamanders and frogs arose from a common ancestor and that the caecilians evolved independently).

The earliest frog-like fossil is a creature known as *Triadobatrachus*, which measures about 10 cm, has a wide, flat skull (as modern frogs do) and a short tail. It seems to have been either an aquatic species or a metamorphosing tadpole (although its skeleton is completely formed), and it was found in deposits dating from the early Triassic period (about 220–230 million years ago) on Madagascar. It is placed in the order Proanura, i.e. 'before frogs', of which it is the only known member.

After *Triadobatrachus* there is an enormous gap of 50–60 million years before the next fossil frogs appear. These belong to species recognisable as frogs and therefore to the order Anura. It seems, then, that frogs similar to some of the species which are extant today were living about 150 million years ago. The surviving members of that group are in the families Leiopelmatidae and Discoglossidae, collectively known as the sub-order Archeobatrachidae ('ancient frogs'). The Pipidae, Rhinophrynidae, Pelobatidae and Pelodytidae, together with an extinct form, Paleobatrachidae, are sometimes included in this order, and sometimes grouped together as the sub-order Mesobatrachia ('middle frogs'). Fossil frogs belonging to this assemblage of families are known from Israel, dating from about 100–135 million years ago (Cretaceous period). All of the remaining families of frogs are more recently evolved, and are placed in the sub-order Neobatrachia ('new frogs'), their oldest known fossils being a 'mere' fifty million years old!

Chapter 2
Design – size, shape and colour

The roughly 3,500 species of frogs and toads all differ, however slightly, in their appearance. In addition, several species occur in more than one distinct form, sometimes geographically separated (in which case a number of sub-species may be recognised), and sometimes through the existence of several colour 'phases' within a population. Each species has evolved into its present form through selective pressures which allow only those individuals best suited to prevailing conditions to thrive – survival of the fittest. In order to overcome the problems of changing conditions, or to colonise fresh areas, species must adapt, and these adaptations are responsible for the great diversity of size, shape and colour within the anurans (behavioural adaptations have also taken place and these will be dealt with in other parts of this book).

Size

The largest frog in the world is probably *Conraua goliath*, the Goliath frog from West Africa, which may exceed 300 mm in length (frogs are measured from the tip of their snout to their vent), although an as yet undescribed frog from the highlands of New Guinea, known to the local tribesmen as 'carn-pnay' may exceed even this. In North America, the Colorado River toad, *Bufo alvarius*, grows to 150 cm, as does the bullfrog, *Rana catesbeiana* (plate 4); in South America, two toads, *Bufo blombergi* and *Bufo paracnemis* (the rococo toad), grow to 250 mm and 210 mm respectively. In Asia, *Bufo asper* (plate 5) may reach 215 mm; the African bullfrog, *Pyxicephalus adspersus* (plate 7), grows to about 200 mm; in Australia the largest native species is *Mixophytes iteratus*, the giant barred frog, although the naturalised *Bufo marinus* (plate 74), exceeds this comfortably at 150 mm; and in Europe, the common toad, *Bufo bufo*, sometimes reaches 150 mm in the south of its range. Generally speaking, female frogs and toads are bigger than males, but there are exceptions.

There must be many contenders for the 'smallest frog' title, including several *Eleutherodactylus* spp. (e.g. plate 6), and microhylids, some of which measure only slightly more than 10 mm in length, while *Sminthillus limbatus* from Cuba is so small at around 11.5 mm that it is said to produce only one egg at a time. *Psyllophryne didactyla*, from Brazil (Brachycephalidae), however, is currently reckoned to be the smallest species – 9.8 mm!

Most frogs fall within the size range 20–80 mm, but life-style has a bearing on size, as, for instance, tree frogs must necessarily be smaller

Plate 4   North America's largest anuran, the well-known bullfrog, *Rana catesbeiana*.

Plate 5   *Bufo asper*, a forest toad, is the largest species in Asia.

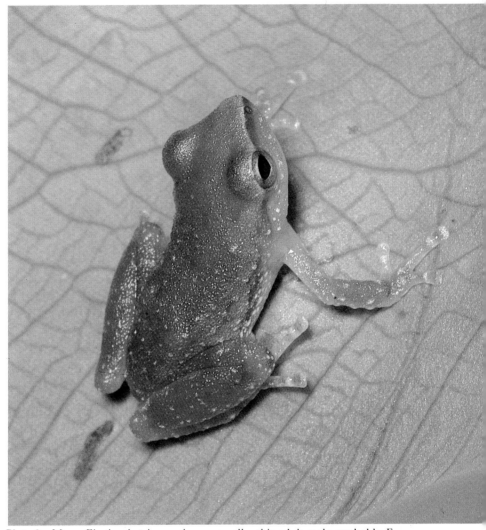

Plate 6   Many *Eleutherodactylus* species are small – this adult male, probably *E. acuminatus*, measured little more than 15 mm.

(on average) than terrestrial frogs in order to climb and support themselves on smooth surfaces and thin branches.

Shape

Frogs and toads are not all the same shape. This rather obvious observation leads us to ask why certain characteristics are present in some species but not in others, and the various answers can be summed up in

Plate 7 *Pyxicephalus adspersus* is Africa's version of the bullfrog. It is not especially long, but has a girth which more than compensates.

the term 'adaptations to the environment'. Thus frogs which rely heavily on their ability to leap, whether to catch food or to avoid being eaten themselves, have long powerful hind legs, whereas those species which are more sedentary (often known popularly as toads) have short hind legs. Similarly, species which swim a lot are streamlined in shape and have large, heavily webbed back feet, whereas the more terrestrial kinds may be rotund in shape with little or no webbing between their toes.

We might say that the 'design' of a species is made up of a set of adaptations, each equipping its owner for life amongst various environmental pressures which exist in its habitat. Many of these are associated with feeding, defence and breeding, and are dealt with more fully under those headings, but other factors are also involved and these will be examined here.

Eyes

Most frogs are nocturnal and, in keeping with this, they have pupils which close down to a slit when exposed to bright light, in order to protect the sensitive cells of the retina (but note that this may not be obvious, because many of these species have dark irises which may obscure the shape of the pupil). The slit may be vertically or, less

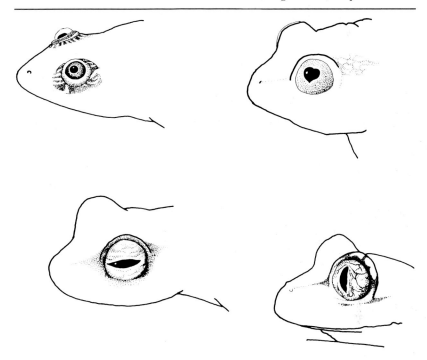

Fig. 2 Pupil shape in frogs: round, heart-shaped, horizontally elliptical and vertically elliptical.

commonly, horizontally, positioned, a feature which is often useful in identifying families of frogs. For example, horizontal pupils are found in frogs belonging to the following families: Bufonidae; Dendrobatidae; Centrolenidae; Ranidae and Rhacophoridae, whereas the Pelobatidae and Leptodactylidae have vertical pupils. Some families, e.g. Hyperoliidae and Hylidae, contain members which may have either type. Round pupils are found in two families, the Pipidae and the Microhylidae. The discoglossids (fire-bellied toads, etc.) are unusual in having triangular or heart-shaped pupils, with the exception of the midwife toads, *Alytes*, which have vertical pupils.

Some frogs (notably the ranids and hylids), have a 'third eyelid', known as the nictitating membrane, which can be drawn up over the eye in order to protect it, while still allowing a limited amount of vision. It is often intricately reticulated in pattern and may be brightly coloured (plate 8).

Ears

One of the most interesting aspects of frogs' biology is their ability to vocalise. It follows that they also need a well-developed sense of hearing.

Plate 8   The nictitating membrane of some species, for example *Hyla geographica*, is elaborately reticulated. Note that the pupil can be seen beneath the membrane, indicating that the frog is not totally unsighted.

The structure of the ear is hidden beneath the skin at a point just behind the eye, but its site may be marked by the presence of an external ear-drum, or tympanum, which is present in many species. It is most obvious in smooth-skinned frogs such as members of the Ranidae, and it is interesting to note that there may be a marked difference in the size of the tympanum between the sexes, that of the male being about twice the size of that of the female in the American bullfrog, for instance.

Limbs

It is in the size and shape of the limbs that adaptations to particular life-styles are best demonstrated. Most species that climb have digits which terminate in expanded discs which enable them to cling to branches, leaves and smooth, slippery surfaces. The best known exponents of this modification are found amongst the various species of 'tree frogs' – the members of the families Hylidae, Rhacophoridae, Hyperoliidae and Centrolenidae, but groups of species from several other families have also evolved along similar lines if their habitats have demanded it. Several ranids have adhesive toe-pads, sometimes for climbing amongst

Plate 9   The adhesive pads can be seen clearly in this *Hyla meridionalis* clinging to a piece of glass. Note also that the skin of the belly is pressed to the surface, improving the adhesion still further.

vegetation but also for clinging to wet boulders alongside streams or beneath waterfalls, where many species live. Amongst the microhylids, the arboreal species of Madagascar also have toe-pads, and in South America, some poison-dart frogs of the family Dendrobatidae are similarly equipped. It is worth noting that although the discs of the above groups of frogs are similar in appearance and function, the internal arrangement of bones and cartilages which gives them their structure differs from one family to another as a result of their separate ancestries.

An extreme case of this parallel evolution exists between the 'flying'

23

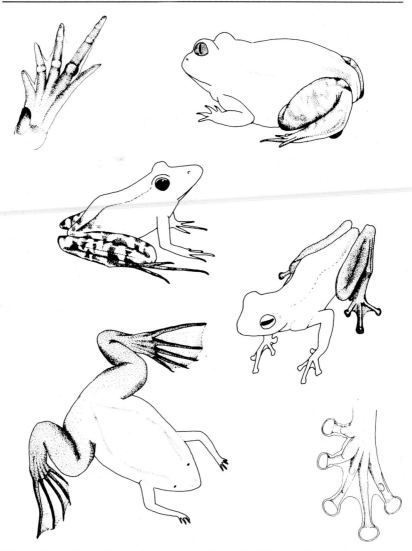

Fig. 3   Adaptive radiation demonstrated in the hind limbs of frogs, showing modifications for burrowing, leaping, climbing and swimming.

frogs: species belonging to the genera *Hyla* (e.g. *Hyla miliaris*) and certain *Agalychnis* species from Central America, and to *Rhacophorus* (e.g. *Rhacophorus reinwardtii* and *R. nigropalmatus*, plate 12) from South East Asia, all have heavily webbed feet which they can spread widely and so glide or parachute from the high branches of the rain forests in which they live. (This strategy has evolved as a means of escaping from predators – the frogs rarely launch themselves unless pursued.)

Plate 10 and Plate 11   Stages in burrowing in the western spadefoot toad, *Scaphiopus hammondi.*

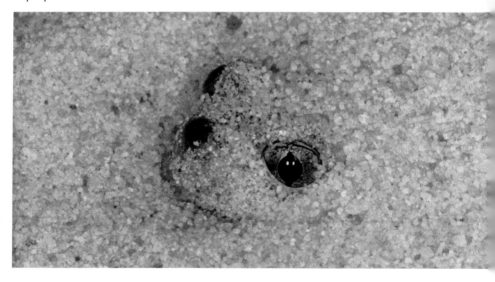

Moving from the tree-tops to below the ground, we can see a further limb modification, this time confined to the hind limbs. Burrowing frogs have a bony tubercle or 'spade' on the outside edge of their feet, the purpose of which is to excavate the soil as they shuffle backwards

Plate 12   *Rhacophorus nigropalmatus* from Borneo. The extensively webbed hands and feet enable the frog to glide from high trees, etc.

beneath the surface (plates 10 and 11). The Pelobatidae, popularly known as 'spadefoot toads', are the obvious examples but, again, frogs from different families, for example the Bufonidae and the single species comprising the Rhinophrynidae, *Rhinophrynus dorsalis*, also have a similar structure. Strangely, there is also a species of 'tree frog', *Pternohyla fodiens*, from the arid south west of North America, which digs its way into the ground using a spade – despite its ancestry amongst the hylids, its adaptations parallel those of species which are unrelated but which have had a similar problem to solve. Note that some frogs burrow head first and these do not possess a spade, but may have powerful front limbs and their skulls may be heavily reinforced.

Among the aquatic frogs, the most obvious limb adaptation is the enlargement of the heavily webbed back feet, with which they thrust themselves through the water, as in *Xenopus* and *Pipa* species, but another structure is found in *Pipa*, in which the digits of the front limbs terminate

Plate 13   The digits of *Pipa pipa* terminate in small star-shaped appendages which probably help it to locate prey.

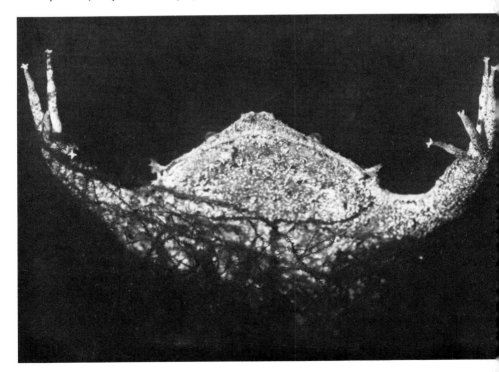

in small star-shaped appendages. These appear to function as sensitive tactile organs, helping the frog to find its way about and, more importantly, to detect food in the murky swamps and pools in which it lives.

Other structures

One of the strangest adornments is the frill of hair-like papillae growing from the dorso-lateral ridges and the inside of the thighs of the male 'hairy' frog, *Trichobatrachus robustus*, at certain times of the year. This species inhabits fast-flowing mountain streams in West Africa, and the hairs are actually threads of skin which serve to increase the surface area over which oxygen can be absorbed from the water. The Lake Titicaca frog, *Telmatobius culeus*, has large baggy folds of skin which serve the same purpose but in this species both sexes are identically modified. A more detailed account of this adaptation is given in the section on respiration, Chapter 3.

Tadpoles

So far we have only considered morphological modifications to adult frogs and toads, but tadpoles are also subject to environmental pressures and have adapted to them. Broadly speaking, tadpoles which live in ponds and other quiet waters have plump bodies and high fins, and tadpoles which live in rivers and streams are more streamlined in shape with long tails and low fins. Within these categories a number of more specialised forms can be found. Those which live in waterfalls and torrents are faced with the problem of maintaining their position while feeding (otherwise they would end up miles downstream). To this end, many species have mouths which are modified into a sucker-like disc. Examples are found in several families: *Heleophryne* species (Heleophrynidae) from southern Africa; *Megistolotis lignarius* (Myobatrachidae) from Australia, and *Bufo perreti* (Bufonidae) from Nigeria, for instance. Some species have gone a stage further and, in addition to the sucker-like mouth, have an abdominal disc which increases their adhesion. These species include the hairy frog, *Trichobatrachus robustus* (Hyperoliidae) from West Africa; the *Amolops* species (Ranidae) from South East Asia (plate 63); and the *Atelopus* and *Ansonia* species (Bufonidae) from South America and South East Asia respectively.

Note however that tadpoles' 'designs' also differ according to their feeding habits or their evolutionary relationships, and these classifications are dealt with in Chapters 5 and 7.

Colour

Although most frogs are dull brown or grey in colour, some are more brightly marked, and these species are often the ones which stimulate our interest in the group (they are also the ones which are most frequently illustrated in popular books!). These markings have not evolved for

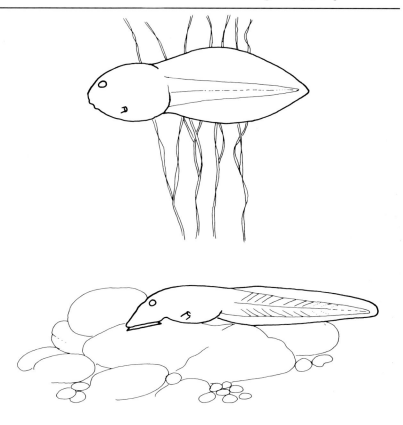

Fig. 4   Typical tadpole shapes: round-bodied pond-dwelling type and flattened stream-dwelling type with sucker-like mouth.

our enjoyment or admiration, however – the colour of every animal has a high survival value: it can enable it to blend into its surroundings; warn predators that it is poisonous or distasteful; help it to absorb or reflect heat, and to identify itself for the purposes of establishing a territory and attracting a mate.

In frogs, colour is produced in two basic ways. In the simplest, pigments are distributed throughout the upper layer of the skin (the epidermis) or between it and a deeper layer (the dermis). In the other type of coloration light is reflected from specialised cells containing a different type of pigment – these cells are located in the dermis.

The pigmentary cells (collectively known as chromatophores) found in frogs fall into three categories:

Melanophores,   containing melanins and related pigments and which give rise to black, brown or red colours.

29

Plate 14   Albinos, such as this leopard frog, are the results of mutations: few reach maturity because they make easy targets for predators.

Xanthophores,   containing carotenoids and pterines, producing yellow, orange or red coloration.

Iridophores,   containing purines, which do not produce a colour in themselves but which reflect light in a special way.

Pigment in the melanophores may be evenly distributed throughout the cell, or contracted into its centre. Since the cells are irregularly branched and overlay each other in a complex lattice arrangement, the frog is able to change its colour from dark to light by dispersing or contracting the pigment granules within each cell. The factors affecting the movement of pigment within the chromatophores are temperature and humidity – warmth and dryness result in contraction of the pigment, making the frog appear pale; cold and dampness cause the pigment to disperse, making the frog appear darker (this is why hibernating frogs are invari-

Plate 15   *Agalychnis callidryas,* the red-eyed tree frog from Central America.

ably dark when discovered). Dispersal of the pigment granules is controlled by the pituitary gland, which produces a melanophore-stimulating hormone (MSH) under certain conditions.

The pigments found in the xanthophores do not appear to be mobile to the same extent as those contained in melanophores, but may vary in intensity due to their origin: these pigments are not produced by the frog but are accumulated from its food. Animals which have red areas of skin normally may lose this colour if they are deprived of their natural source of the pigment – captive-reared fire-bellied toads, *Bombina orientalis*, demonstrate this phenomenon very well: young animals reared on flies or crickets have pale yellow bellies unless they are also provided with an extract containing carotin, but if their natural diet, which includes small crustaceans, is given, the red colour develops without the need of additional supplements.

The Iridophores are found in a deeper layer than either melanophores or xanthophores. The green colour of frogs is produced by light striking these cells and being reflected in such a way as to produce a blue effect, much as small particles in the earth's atmosphere cause the sky to appear blue. This is known as 'Tyndall scattering' after the scientist who first noticed it. In frogs the iridophore is overlaid by a layer of yellow xanthophores and these filter the blue light to produce the familiar green coloration.

Mutations in which the upper xanthophore layer is missing occur very occasionally in nature, resulting in blue frogs. Some species in which this mutation has been observed include the American *Rana clamitans*, the Australasian *Litoria caerulea* and, especially, the Eurasian *Hyla arborea*. Attempts to produce blue offspring from these individuals by selective breeding in the laboratory have so far failed, indicating that the lack of xanthophores is not a heritable trait. Coincidentally, *Litoria caerulea* was named for its blue colour (*caerulea* means blue), not because of an odd mutation but because the species was first described from a specimen in which the preservative had dissolved away the yellow pigment.

Other mutations involve the absence of all of the pigments: these animals appear white or pale pink and are known as albinos; and others in which there is an excess of black pigment: these are known as melanistic animals and are totally or partially black. Normally, such mutations are easily picked out by predators and do not survive long enough to breed and pass on their abnormal genes, and so they occur only rarely (but often attract considerable attention when they do).

In a subsequent chapter we will see how the various colours and their arrangements are used by frogs as a means of defence, but there are other aspects of their colour which are not so easily explained. For instance, the eyes of some species, two of which are illustrated (plates 15 and 80), are bright red, a colour which does not fit in well with the usual idea of camouflage. It may be significant that a red pigment, rhodopsin, is found in the end segment of the rod cells in the retina of vertebrates' eyes, and *Agalychnis* frogs, at least, are thought to have exceptional night vision.

Fig. 5   Polymorphism: striped, speckled and plain individuals may be found in the same population of a species, e.g. *Hyperolius marmoratus*.

Slightly easier to account for is the phenomenon of polymorphism. In several species two or more colour 'phases' occur. Sometimes this situation is further complicated by a number of species existing side by side and all sharing the same phases. A good example of this 'parallel polymorphism' is found amongst the African reed frogs, *Hyperolius*. A number of species of these small frogs have, for example, striped, speckled and plain-coloured individuals within the same population. Thus two striped frogs from the same pond may belong to different species, but a striped, a speckled and a plain one may be the same! A similar situation is found amongst some of the marsupial frogs, *Gastrotheca*, in the Andes of Ecuador and Peru, while in South East Asia a number of frogs belonging to the genus *Rana* (including *R. doriae, R. kuhlii, R. limnocharis, R. nitida* and *R. plicatella*) occur in a plain form as well as in a form with a white or yellow vertebral stripe. A striped example of *R. doriae* is shown in plate 19.

Polymorphism in other animals has been well studied. One conclusion of the research is that the existence of two patterns tends to confuse

33

predators, who find it less easy to 'get their eye in' – this would seem to be a valid explanation, since when searching for frogs a human's success rate tends to increase after the first two or three of a particular kind are found and a 'search-image' has been formed. Perhaps the striped animals escape the notice of a predator which has a search image of the plain ones and vice versa, so encouraging the existence of more than one type within the population. In this way a number of species may combine similar types of polymorphism to their mutual advantage.

Sexual dimorphism, i.e. a difference in markings between the two sexes of a species, is common in insects, fishes and birds but is not nearly so common amongst frogs. The reason for this is that in the groups mentioned, visual display is an important part of territory defence and mate attraction, and the bright colours of the males serve to advertise his ownership or eligibility, whereas frogs, being mostly nocturnal, achieve the same thing by calling. There are a few examples of sexual dimorphism involving colour, however, notably amongst toads of the genus *Bufo*. In the following species the males are more or less uniformly coloured but the females are covered with dark blotches: *Bufo canorus* (Yosemite toad), *Bufo kavirensis* and *Bufo pereglenes*. The latter species is quite remarkable in its coloration: whereas most toads are dull in colour, males of this species are a uniform golden orange and the females are deep red with large brown blotches, the bright colours of the males apparently improving their chances of being found by females in the dark cloud forests of Costa Rica where they live. A similar difference in markings is found in Couch's spadefoot toads (*Scaphiopus couchi*) and in the African *Hyperolius hieroglyphicus* the male is black with yellow reticulations but the female is bright green with yellow dorsolateral stripes.

In most species of frogs and toads the juveniles are small versions of the adults but occasionally they have entirely different colours or markings. This may involve an over-all colour change when sexual maturity is reached, as in *Hyperolius marmoratus*, in which the juveniles are plain brown in colour but the adults are cream and black, or it may involve gradual changes in the shape and/or colour of the markings. For example, in the poison dart frog *Dendrobates leucomelas* the young are primarily black with a broad band of bright yellow around their middles, but as they grow, black spots develop within the yellow area and the markings become progressively more intricate. In another example, the barking frog, *Hylactophryne augusti*, from North America, the juveniles have a prominent white band around the body but this gradually fades until, in the adult form, the frog is a more uniform colour over all.

Chapter 3
Physiology – interior design and function

Whatever their external differences, all frogs and toads function through a number of separate, but mutually dependent, physiological systems. Some of these are quite complex and may seem of little importance to

Plate 16 A preserved frog in which the soft parts have been cleared and the bones stained with alizarin red. In this way the skeletal structure of even delicate specimens, such as this juvenile *Rana plicatella*, can be studied. Note the lack of ribs and the broad head.

the naturalist, but a basic knowledge of them is essential as they have considerable bearing on the way in which frogs behave.

Skin

Since all of the other organs and tissue are wrapped up in the skin it seems logical to begin by looking at this in detail. In amphibians, the skin plays a far more important role than in other vertebrates, as it is responsible, among other things, for water balance and respiration. The structure of the skin comprises two layers: an outer one, known as the epidermis, and an inner one, known as the dermis. Within these layers are a number of specialised cells. Chromatophores, the cells which control the colour of the frog, are situated in either layer depending on their type, and are described in detail on page 29. Other cells aggregate to form glands of two main types: mucus glands, which keep the skin moist and enable gaseous exchange to take place, and poison glands, which secrete the toxins with which many species defend themselves – it is the aggregations of these glands which form the warts and the enlarged parotid glands on toads, etc. Other glands are very localised and

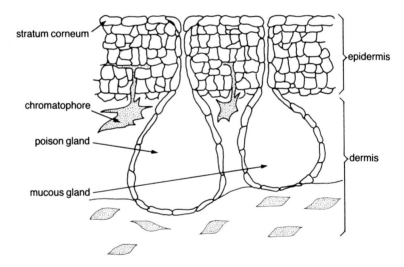

Fig. 6   Diagrammatic representation of a section through frog skin.

include those which secrete mucus onto the pads of tree frogs and so improve their climbing abilities, and those which aggregate to form the nuptial pads which help the males to grasp females during amplexus.

In some areas of the skin which are not glandular, the epidermis becomes cornified, to form, for instance, the 'spades' on the hind feet of many burrowing species and the beak-like mouth-parts of tadpoles.

When frogs shed their skin, which may be as often as every few days, it is the outermost, dead, layer of the epidermis (known as the *stratum corneum*) which comes away and, in the majority of species, it is immediately eaten – in fact the frog pulls the skin away from its body with its mouth, swallowing it as it does so.

Respiration

Respiration is the process by which animals take up oxygen and give off carbon dioxide. In frogs and toads this may be done in a combination of ways: all adults have functional lungs, but the larval stages breathe by means of gills – in fact, the evolution of frogs from fishes is, in a simplified way, re-enacted with each generation of frogs. In addition to their lungs or gills, both adults and larvae absorb oxygen through their skin, either from the water or from the air.

The lungs of adult frogs are paired and each consists of a 'bag' containing many folds of tissue lined with small chambers (alveoli) in which gaseous exchange takes place, i.e. oxygen passes from the air into the bloodstream via small, thin-walled blood vessels (capillaries), and carbon dioxide passes in the other direction. The lung is not muscular as it is in mammals, for instance, but air is pumped in and out of it by raising and lowering the floor of the mouth – this can be observed in a resting frog by watching the regular movements of its throat.

The gills of tadpoles are also paired, but each is divided into at least three branches. These branch again to form a feathery tangle of filaments, each well-served with capillaries, which exchange the waste carbon dioxide for oxygen. In most newly hatched tadpoles these gills are visible outside the body but they are soon covered over as a flap of skin grows back from the 'cheek' region, forming a chamber around them. Water is pumped into each chamber and, having passed over the gill filaments, exits through an opening known as the spiracle. In the majority of species the chambers are connected internally and share a common spiracle, but in primitive species such as *Xenopus* there are two spiracles, one for each gill system (see also page 100). Just before metamorphosis, the frog begins to develop lungs and the gills degenerate.

The third method of respiration, through the skin, is carried out by larval and adult frogs. Oxygen and carbon dioxide are passed into and out of the bloodstream via capillaries which run very close to the skin's surface. In adult terrestrial frogs this is possible only if the skin is moist and is the reason for its wet and slimy coating, and also for frogs' preference for humid habitats – those species which live in dry places are unable to breathe effectively through their skin and need larger and more efficient lungs as a result. Tadpoles may obtain over half of their oxygen by this 'cutaneous respiration' but adult frogs usually obtain less, perhaps a quarter, depending on their environment. A few species, however, seem to have gone to great lengths to exploit this source of oxygen, the most efficient being the Lake Titicaca frog, *Telmatobius culeus*. This species is totally aquatic and its skin consists of so many wrinkles and folds that it looks as though it should contain a much bigger frog.

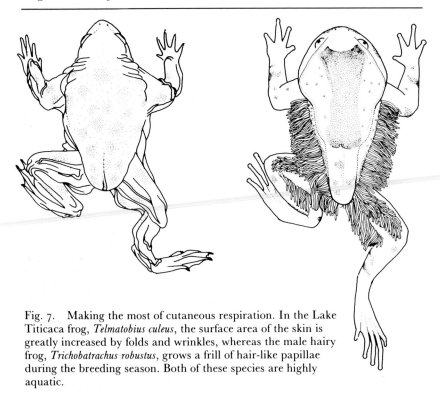

Fig. 7.   Making the most of cutaneous respiration. In the Lake Titicaca frog, *Telmatobius culeus*, the surface area of the skin is greatly increased by folds and wrinkles, whereas the male hairy frog, *Trichobatrachus robustus*, grows a frill of hair-like papillae during the breeding season. Both of these species are highly aquatic.

The purpose of this bizarre piece of evolution is greatly to increase the surface area of the skin and thus the area over which oxygen can diffuse, enabling the frog to remain beneath the surface for the whole of its life if necessary. It seems likely that this adaptation is a result of the rarefied air which exists at the high altitude where they live, coupled with the high oxygen level in the cold water of the lake. Other high-altitude species of *Telmatobius*, e.g. *T. patagonicus*, are similarly endowed with extra skin but to a lesser degree, whereas lowland species are not.

The hair-like papillae which grow from parts of the frog *Trichobatrachus robustus* serve a similar purpose but are confined to the male. It has been suggested that only he possesses the 'hairs' because he moves around beneath the surface searching for females during the breeding season and/or that he remains with his clutch of eggs which are laid on the stream bed. By increasing his oxygen intake from the water he does not need to abandon his duties so often in order to take air at the surface. In this species, the rapidly flowing waters of the mountain streams in which the frog lives pass over the hairs, continually bringing fresh oxygen to it, but because *Telmatobius* lives in still water it must agitate its folds and flaps constantly in order to prevent an oxygen-depleted 'water jacket' forming around it. Moreover, it appears that in all frogs, the flow of blood to the capillaries near the skin's surface can be regulated on a second to second basis according to the requirements of the animal or the oxygen capacity of the air or water with which it is in contact.

Circulatory system

The circulatory system carries the materials needed for metabolism to the parts of the body where they can be used, and also removes the waste products of metabolism away from these cells, and transfers them to areas where they can be disposed of, such as the kidneys. It is also used as a route for distributing hormones around the body and for carrying the cells which fight bacterial infection.

Amphibians were the first animals to evolve a double circulatory system, one part of which passes blood through the lungs, where gaseous exchange takes place through the thin-walled capillaries, dumping carbon dioxide and collecting oxygen, and the other part of which takes oxygenated blood to various parts of the body which absorb the oxygen (and other substances if present). The two systems come together in the three-chambered heart. The upper left chamber receives the oxygenated blood from the lungs and passes it to the lower chamber, from which it is pumped, via a system of arteries, around the body. Part of this system passes around the gut and transports the substances absorbed there to the liver, where they are either stored or returned to the blood for further distribution. Blood which has passed around the body becomes de-oxygenated and returns to the upper right chamber of the heart – it then passes back into the lower chamber and is pumped once more to the lungs. The lower chamber is therefore common to both circuits, but in fact the oxygenated blood is kept separate from the de-oxygenated blood by a pattern of muscular strands which keep blood coming from the right separate from that coming from the left.

Endocrine system

The endocrine system is concerned with the ductless glands, which secrete hormones and control, to a large extent, the animal's behaviour. They are situated in various parts of its anatomy and the functions of the glands are of great interest to the naturalist. The two most important endocrine glands are the thyroid and the pituitary.

In frogs, the paired thyroid glands are situated in the throat region and their most important function is to control metamorphosis. In the absence of thyroid glands, a tadpole would continue to grow but would fail to metamorphose into its adult form. On the other hand, if extra thyroid extract is given experimentally to a tadpole, it will metamorphose quickly, even if it is smaller than normal. Under natural conditions, the functioning of the thyroid can be inhibited by cold temperatures: tadpoles which live in cold water metamorphose at a relatively large size (in comparison with their ultimate adult size) than species which live in warm water – this may have some survival value since the warmest water is often associated with shallow pools which are more likely to dry up completely in a short period of time (e.g. dune slacks, rain pools in deserts, etc.) and, in these situations, rapid metamorphosis is more important than size at metamorphosis. Hormones from the thyroid glands also stimulate skin shedding.

The pituitary gland is situated at the base of the brain, to which it is attached. It produces a number of different hormones, some of which control secretions from other endocrine glands: for instance, thyroid stimulating hormone (TSH), and hormones which stimulate egg or sperm production in the ovary or testes (FSH and LH). Melanophore stimulating hormone has already been mentioned as it controls colour change in frogs by causing melanin granules to contract or disperse in their cells (see page 32), while other hormones control migration to the breeding sites and other reproductive behaviour. Yet another hormone from the pituitary, vasotocin, is concerned with the frog's ability to maintain a correct water balance between its body and the environment.

Reproductive system

The reproductive system comprises the ovaries in female or the testes in male frogs, and the various tubes and ducts which transport the eggs or sperm. The female has a pair of ovaries which lie alongside the kidneys. Each is associated with a fat body which stores the nutrients necessary for the formation of the eggs. When the female is in a reproductive state, the ovaries will be full of eggs, sometimes numbering several thousand and the fat bodies will be small; at the end of the breeding season, the ovaries will be empty, and the fat bodies will begin to swell again in preparation for the next breeding season. The accumulated eggs are released from the ovary prior to spawning and enter the oviduct via a funnel-shaped structure at its open end (the ostia). They then pass along the highly coiled oviduct where glands situated in its lining coat them with the clear gelatinous 'jelly' which is typical of amphibian eggs. The lower end of each oviduct expands into a uterus, a chamber where the eggs are stored for a short time immediately prior to spawning. The two uteri open into the cloaca, from which they are expelled during spawning.

The male has a pair of testes which, like the ovaries, lie alongside the kidneys and which are associated with fat bodies from which they obtain the necessary materials for sperm production. Each testis is connected by a series of small ducts to a larger one, the Wolffian duct, which has the dual purpose of transporting the sperm and draining the kidneys. Sperm which has passed down this duct is stored temporarily in the seminal vesicle, a short, widened zone at its lower end which connects with the cloaca. The seminal vesicles and the testes are largest during the breeding season and shrink noticeably when this is over. Some species, however, do not show any seasonal pattern in this respect but continue to produce sperm (and eggs in the case of females) throughout the year. This sometimes occurs in response to a permanently cold environment, such as mountain streams and lakes – the formation of these cells takes such a long time under these conditions that year-round activity of the reproductive organs is necessary if they are to achieve their full reproductive potential.

Otherwise, the production of eggs or sperm, and the fluctuating size of the various components which comprise the male and female reproductive systems are controlled by hormones, the secretion of which is in turn controlled by a variety of environmental stimuli such as temperature, daylength, rainfall and food supply.

Water balance

Animals need to maintain a certain amount of water within their cells at all times. Frogs and toads, whose total body weight includes as much as 80 per cent of water, do not drink, but absorb water from their surroundings through their skin by a process known as osmosis. Aquatic species and tadpoles must limit the amount of water retained in their bodies, while terrestrial species must limit the amount passing out. The most important means of regulating water balance is by controlling the amount of water absorbed through the skin against the amount excreted through the kidney. This is accomplished through hormone secretions coupled, in certain cases, with various physiological and behavioural adaptations. Thus, tadpoles and frogs living in water excrete large volumes of urine, consisting mainly of ammonia, in order to eliminate surplus water from their bodies, but terrestrial adults need to retain as much water as possible by getting rid of their waste products as urea – a substance which is not so toxic and can therefore be stored up and excreted at intervals with the minimum amount of water. For example, aquatic species such as *Pipa pipa* excrete about 90 per cent of their waste nitrogen as ammonia, whereas in terrestrial species such as *Bufo* the proportion is reduced to about 5 per cent, the rest being urea. At least one species, the African grey tree frog, *Chiromantis xerampelina*, which lives in a very arid environment, has gone one better by excreting *its* waste as uric acid, a white paste requiring almost no water to carry it out of the body – a system which is usually associated with birds and reptiles, which are well known for their frugal use of water.

Because most frogs breathe through their skin, it follows that this surface will also be susceptible to water loss, although species which live in very dry places have a more impermeable layer of tissue within the dermis and therefore rely more heavily on their lungs for respiration. Furthermore, in many species the skin is more glandular and therefore moister on the ventral surface than on the dorsal – this enables them to breathe through the ventral part of their skin, but to reduce water loss during periods of dry conditions by crouching close to the substrate and gathering their limbs in to their bodies. At least two species, including the *Chiromantis* species mentioned above and an Argentinian hylid, *Phyllomedusa sauvagei*, secrete a waxy substance and use their hind limbs to smear it over the whole of their bodies, so forming a coating which considerably reduces evaporation. The *Phyllomedusa* produces this fluid

Plate 17   Frog skin is normally kept moist at all times by means of thousands of small glands in the dermis.

from glands in its parotid region, but the source in *Chiromantis* is not known.

Several of the burrowing frogs which are restricted to arid regions are able to resist drought by forming a cocoon around their bodies when they become dry. This consists of several layers of their outer skin (*stratum corneum*) which are sloughed together, but which remain in place around the animal until damp conditions prevail, when they break free of this covering (and eat it). Species in which this type of behaviour has been recorded belong to at least five families and live in four distinct dry regions in different parts of the world:

Northern Argentina: *Ceratophrys ornata, Lepidobatrachus llanensis* (Leptodactylidae).

Australia: *Cyclorana alboguttatus, C. platycephalus, C. australis, Limnodynastes spenceri, Neobatrachus pictus* (Myobatrachidae).

Africa: *Pyxicephalus adspersus,* (Ranidae), *Leptopelis bocagei* (Hyperoliidae).

Mexico – Arizona: *Pternohyla fodiens* (Hylidae).

If all else fails, many of the drought-adapted species are able to withstand a remarkably high degree of desiccation: spadefoot toads and some *Bufo* species can lose almost half of their total body weight due to evaporation whereas species from typically humid environments would succumb long before this stage is reached. An additional advantage which drought-adapted species have is the ability to absorb water much faster than other species.

Thermoregulation

Like fishes and reptiles, all amphibians are ectotherms – this means that they are not able to raise their body temperature by producing metabolic heat (only birds and mammals can do this), but must rely on outside sources of heat to warm them up. The temperatures at which they function best range from 20 to 30°C, the exact value depending on species, each of which has an optimum body temperature. Below this optimum, or preferred, temperature, bodily functions such as digestion, respiration and spermatogenesis slow down and movement becomes progressively more sluggish. At the lower extreme, a critical minimum temperature is reached when the animal is unable to move at all (and is therefore unable to search for a more favourable environment), whereas the upper limit is known as the critical maximum temperature, at which the frog also loses the power of locomotion and will eventually die of heat exhaustion.

For frogs as a whole these critical limits are reached at about 3°C and 40°C – the highest recorded body temperatures are found in a tropical toad, *Bufo marinus*, while a small temperate frog, *Acris crepitans*, can operate at 35°C. These are extremes, however, and most species seem to be happiest at 20–25°C, which coincides with the ambient temperature in many parts of the tropics and sub-tropics and so the frogs living in these regions need to do little or nothing in order to maintain a satisfactory temperature throughout the year. In temperate regions it may be necessary for frogs to hibernate underground for some of the year in order to avoid lethal temperatures on the surface, whereas in deserts a reversal of this situation takes place – frogs are active during the cooler parts of the year and burrow to avoid lethally high temperatures during the summer, a process known as aestivation. Similarly, frogs' diurnal rhythm may be geared to temperature, although other factors, notably predation, may affect this.

Although it is widely accepted that frogs do not actively thermoregulate in the same way as, say, lizards, but tend to work within the limitations imposed on them by the temperatures of their surroundings, some species certainly do manage to raise their body temperatures by basking. Because of the problem of dehydration, however, basking is mostly restricted to species which live close to the water, into which they can retreat from time to time – the European marsh frog, *Rana ridibunda*, is a good example of this type, and can raise its body temperature several degrees above that of its surroundings by basking.

Tadpoles develop more quickly in warm water and it is not unusual to find that they congregate at the edges of ponds where the water is shallow and therefore warmer – indeed, many species of frogs, especially those living in cool places, e.g. the natterjack toad, *Bufo calamita*, select shallow pools in which to spawn (although this issue may be affected by the fact that small bodies of water, especially if they are temporary, are less likely to contain predators).

Chapter 4
Staying Alive: enemies and defence

Frogs and toads appear on the menu of a huge array of other animals. Their more obvious enemies include snakes, many of which prey exclusively on them, wading birds such as storks and herons, and larger members of their own clan. Other predators include several large invertebrates, especially spiders, fish (which devour eggs and tadpoles as well as adult frogs), turtles, crocodilians, small mammals such as shrews, mustelids, raccoons, etc., and larger mammals.

Other stages in the frog's life-cycle are also vulnerable to predation. Tadpoles are eaten by a variety of animals, including aquatic insects and their nymphs, fishes, newts and their larvae, and other frog larvae. The eggs may contain substances which make them distasteful, and the jelly surrounding them also provides some protection, but again, fish and newts will occasionally prey on them, while eggs that are laid on leaves overhanging pools in Central and South America – for instance, those of the leaf frogs, *Agalychnis* and *Phyllomedusa* species – are regularly eaten by a snake, *Leptodeira annulata*, which specialises in hunting in the bushes which are used by these frogs.

As a race, their main defence against this onslaught is fecundity – frogs and toads produce enormous numbers of eggs, only a fraction of which are required to ensure the continuation of each species, but individually each animal also optimises its chance of survival in a variety of ways. The most effective of these is to escape notice altogether and the majority of frogs and toads are extremely secretive, usually hiding during their period of inactivity beneath rocks, logs, in crevices in trees, or buried in the leaf-litter or soil. Anyone who has seen frogs congregating around a pool at breeding time will have asked himself 'Where do they all go?' since even a thorough search of the surrounding area the following day will only turn up a small proportion of the animals which were present the night before. Many of the others will be tucked away in holes or buried deep beneath the surface, but others will be in full view, resting on vegetation, dead leaves, on the bark of trees or on rocks. To the untrained eye, however, they will be all but invisible owing to their resemblance, both in colour and in texture, to the substrate on which they are resting. As expected, most species which live on the forest floor are brown (e.g. most toads, of the genus *Bufo* and others), those living in sandy places tend towards yellow, and those which rest amongst leaves, reeds, etc., are often bright green (e.g. many tree frogs belonging to the genera *Hyla*, *Litoria*, *Hyperolius*, etc.). Other camouflage patterns include those which resemble lichens, such as *Hyla chrysoscelis* (plate 20) from

Plate 18 *Hyla granosa* from Ecuador is one of many arboreal species in which the green coloration provides camouflage.

Plate 19 A broad vertebral stripe is a common disruptive marking amongst frogs from a number of families. This is *Rana doriae* from Malaysia.

Plate 20 *Hyla chrysoscelis* from North America is beautifully camouflaged when resting on tree-trunks. This species has orange flash-markings on its groin which are visible only when it leaps.

North America and *Litoria nannotis* from Australia, and stripes on frogs which live amongst grass and low vegetation, e.g. the *Kassina* species from Africa. Features which would make them conspicuous, especially their eyes, will be disguised by disruptive markings and in some cases the complete body will be broken up visually by vertebral stripes (see plate 19 for instance), transverse bars or cunningly shaded areas of skin (plate 59).

Furthermore, in order to present an image which is as unfrog-like as possible, many species are decorated with a variety of frills, flaps and appendages which serve to change the shape in subtle ways. A common form of disruptive outline consists of the development of fleshy 'horns' above the eyes and sometimes on the snout of species such as *Megophrys nasuta* from Asia (plate 22), *Ceratophrys cornuta* (plate 23), all five species of *Hemiphractus* (fig. 20) and *Gastrotheca ceratophrys* from South America, *Litoria prora* from Australia, *Ceratobatrachus guentheri* from the Solomon Islands and *Asterophrys turpicula* from New Guinea. These species belong to the families Pelobatidae, Leptodactylidae, Hylidae, Ranidae and Microhylidae, which shows that this arrangement has arisen independently at various times during the frogs' evolution. Other ways of disrupting the outline include small triangles of skin on the ankles of several tree frogs such as *Hyla boans* and *Rhacophorus bimaculatus*, and a frill, or lappet, along the outer edge of the limbs of other tree frogs such as *Hyla lancasteri*, *Rhacophorus appendiculata* and *Litoria eucnemis*. As well as breaking up the outline of the frog, these frills may also help to eliminate the shadow cast by the frog, making it appear less three-dimensional and therefore less conspicuous.

Cryptically marked frogs rely so heavily on their camouflage that they remain immobile until the last possible moment. Only then do they resort to their other great defence strategy, flight, and sometimes they will have yet another trick up their sleeves, or rather under their legs, because several of the camouflaged species expose a patch of brightly marked skin as they straighten their legs and leap away. These 'flash' markings have evolved to confuse predators in the following way: the resting frog decides that the predator is too close for comfort and leaps, at which point the predator's eye is immediately drawn to the bright marking. At the end of the leap this suddenly disappears as the frog lands and folds its legs again, leaving the predator looking for a 'search image' which no longer exists. Examples of camouflaged species which have 'flash' markings are *Hyla chrysoscelis* (plate 20) and *Phyllomedusa tomopterna* (plate 24).

Of course, large numbers of frogs rely entirely on flight, being superbly equipped with long, powerful hind limbs which take them away from danger in one or two great bounds. Species living near the water spend most of their lives within one leap of it, and immediately dive into the mud or debris on the bottom, but some are reluctant to enter the water and make off in the opposite direction – presumably, generations of selective breeding have favoured this behaviour in places where aquatic predators, e.g. fish, are the most common predator. Yet other species

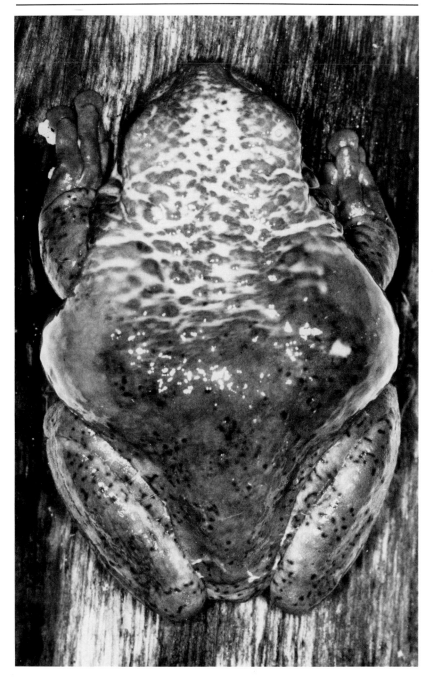

Plate 21   *Phrynohyas venulosa*, a neotropical hylid, exudes a noxious fluid from glands in its skin.

Plate 22   The Asian horned toad, *Megophrys nasuta*, is a classic example of crypsis through disruptive outline.

Plate 23   A number of species which rely on crypsis have prominent horns over their eyes: *Ceratophrys cornuta* is an extreme example.

Plate 24   The flash markings of *Phyllomedusa tomopterna*, an Ecuadorian leaf-folding frog, normally remain hidden.

Plate 25   This leptodactylid, *Pleurodema*, has distinctively marked glands in its lumbar region. Apart from secreting poison, they may be used as eye-spots during an intimidation display (see also fig. 8).

Plate 26   In bufonids and some other groups of frogs, poison glands are heavily concentrated in certain areas, such as in the parotid region of this Colorado River toad, *Bufo alvarius*.

will jump onto the water but continue jumping right across until they reach the middle of the pond or stream, or even the opposite side, behaving in much the same way as a flat pebble skimming across the water's surface.

Despite the effectiveness of hiding and/or fleeing, frogs inevitably come face to face with an enemy occasionally and other defences are necessary. The most important of these is the secretion of toxic or distasteful substances from the skin, an ability shared by many species from a wide range of families. Most frogs are covered with a coating of slimy mucus anyway, and this is often sufficient to prevent their capture, but many also secrete substances known collectively as batrachotoxins, a high concentration of which can be lethal if it enters the bloodstream. There is variation in the exact composition of the toxin, its strength and in the position of the glands which secrete it. These may be fairly evenly distributed over the whole of the animal's skin, as in the tree frog *Phrynohyas venulosa* (*venulosa* means poisonous), or they may be heavily concentrated in certain areas. For instance, in toads of the genus *Bufo*, they form large lumps behind and above the eyes and, sometimes, on the thighs; in some species of *Pleurodema* and in *Cacosternum capense* similar raised areas are found on the lumbar region of the back; and in the genus *Odontophrynus* they are on the shin. If any of these species are molested, a milky fluid oozes from the pores and a taste of this will usually cause a predator to reject it.

The most deadly toxins are produced by the spectacular poison dart frogs, genera *Dendrobates* and *Phyllobates* (plates 27, 38, 92, and 93). These Central and South American frogs, numbering about fifty-five known species altogether, produce, in addition to a very powerful batrachotoxin, a lethal cocktail containing several other alkaloid toxins which, though not as devastating in effect, are unique to this group of frogs, and include histrionicotoxins and pumiliotoxins, named after *Dendrobates histrionicus* and *D. pumilio*, the species from which they were first isolated, but which are also found in other species. This defence system is exploited by a group of Colombian Indians who extract the poison from at least three species for use on their blow darts, hence the common name (see also Chapter 8).

The poison dart frogs are all extravagantly marked, diurnal, and often behave in an unusually bold manner, making little or no attempt to hide or escape. This 'warning' or 'aposematic' coloration and behaviour is associated with poisonous or distasteful species throughout the animal kingdom, but nowhere is its cause and effect as dramatically demonstrated as in the species *Phyllobates terribilis*. This species, which was only described in 1978, hails from western Colombia. In colour it is brilliant yellow or orange and it grows to about 35 mm – quite large for a poison dart frog. Its claim to fame is the exceedingly high concentrations of batrachotoxin and homobatrachotoxin found in its skin – twenty times more toxic than those produced by any other dendrobatid. A single specimen of this species may yield 1,900 micrograms of poison: a mere 2–200 micrograms are thought to be lethal to man! Incredibly, a frog-eating snake, *Leimadophis epinephelus*, is thought to be immune to this toxin and probably constitutes its only predator, apart from the Choco Indians who use its poison to tip their darts.

Several other groups of frogs are brightly marked to warn of poisonous secretions, for example, certain *Atelopus* toads, but very little appears to be known of the strength of the poison or the effectiveness of the warning coloration. Other species produce toxins but are not quite so open about advertising themselves to predators. These may have areas of warning coloration on parts of their bodies which are normally hidden. The fire-bellied toads, *Bombina*, the small South American bufonids in the genus *Dendrophryniscus* and the Australian myobatrachids *Adelotus brevis* and *Metacrinia nichollsi*, for instance, have undersides which are marked with bold blotches of red, orange or yellow, but are cryptically coloured in grey or green above. If disturbed, some of these species arch their backs and raise the palms of their hands and feet to expose the flash colours (plate 28), a behavioural response known as 'Unkenreflex' after the German name for the fire-bellied toad, *Bombina bombina*. In this way they make use of two defensive strategies, crypsis (concealment) and warning coloration, by means of a stereotyped behaviour pattern.

Plate 27 Warning coloration is characteristic of the highly toxic poison dart frogs, such as this *Dendrobates lehmanni*.

Other species of frogs and toads which are not brightly marked may also react in pre-set ways to repel predators. The most common response is to achieve an apparent increase in size by inflating the body, raising it off the ground by straightening the legs, and tilting it towards the attacker. Snakes, which are amongst the most important predators of frogs, may often be discouraged in this way because they are unable to

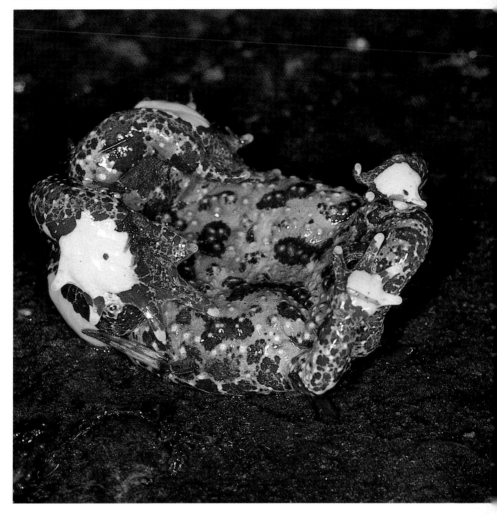

Plate 28 The 'Unkenreflex' of *Bombina variegata* consists of arching the back and raising the hands and feet in order to display as much of the brightly coloured underside as possible.

chew their food and must swallow it whole – here, size is obviously an important factor to be considered when selecting a meal. A number of South American leptodactylids, including *Physalaemus nattereri*, *Telmatobius praebasalticus* and certain *Pleurodema* species, have evolved a bizarre modification to this behaviour. They possess a pair of prominently marked glands, forming ocelli, or eye-spots, on their rumps and, if threatened, will turn away and straighten their back legs, so presenting the predator with a crude, but presumably effective, imitation of the face of a much

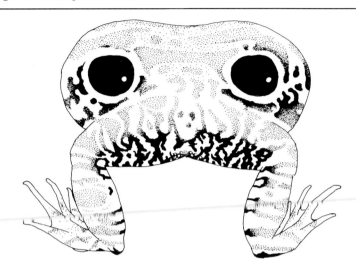

Fig. 8 *Physalaemus nattereri* and a few other leptodactylids have prominent eye-spots or ocelli on their rumps, which they display to intimidate predators.

larger animal (fig. 8) – in each case the frog quite literally turns its back on the problem and puts on a brave face!

Another means of startling or intimidating an attacker is common to many species and consists of screaming loudly when grasped or approached. This distress call can be sufficient to deter a timid or hesitant enemy but would seem unlikely to be effective against snakes, which are, in any case, practically deaf to air-borne sounds.

Other frogs and toads try to avoid being eaten by pretending to be dead. This technique, known as thanatosis, is better documented amongst insects and mammals such as the possum. In frogs it consists of drawing the limbs tightly into the sides of the body and closing the eyes. Other species may hold the limbs rigidly outstretched. If the frog is climbing it may fall to the ground and remain motionless for a minute or more. Thanatosis is probably only effective against animals that prefer to take living prey, and it may also help the frog to escape notice if movement is an important visual clue to the predator involved.

A very specialised predator of frogs is the bat *Trachops cirrhosus* from Central America, which locates male frogs from their mating call. It has learned to recognise the calls of the various species of poisonous frogs which inhabit this region, and concentrates its attention on the tasty ones. Some of these may minimise predation by ceasing to call altogether once a bat has been sighted, e.g. *Physalaemus pustulosus*; by calling at infrequent intervals, e.g. *Eleutherodactylus fitzingeri*; or by tight synchronisation of their calls, e.g. *Smilisca silus*. In the Old World, bats of the genus *Megoderma* also hunt frogs but no one has investigated what avoiding action, if any, is taken.

Finally, there are those species which believe that attack is the best means of defence. Frogs such as *Pyxicephalus adspersus, Ceratophrys* species and the related *Lepidobatrachus* species may open their mouths widely, grunt or scream loudly and lunge at their tormentor, biting hard and repeatedly. Faced with this performance, predators many times larger than the frog, including humans, may reconsider the advisability of interfering with it, and indeed, in parts of South America, *Ceratophrys* toads are regarded as highly poisonous by many local people. All of these species are relatively large but others are smaller, such as the weird hylids belonging to the genus *Hemiphractus*. Of the five known species, three (*H. bubalus, fasciatus,* and *proboscidens*) have been observed to open their mouths and gape widely if disturbed, displaying the bright yellow buccal cavity and tongue, and *H. fasciatus*, at least, will follow this up if necessary by biting hard and holding on for some considerable time, leaving a painful impression of its lower tusks. *Asterophrys turpicula*, a microhylid from New Guinea, exhibits similar behaviour and a number of species belonging to the genus *Leptopelis* from West Africa may also open their mouths widely, tilt their body and half close their eyes if threatened, but this action appears to be bluff as I can find no records of them actually biting. The famous 'hairy' frog, *Trichobatrachus*, has sharp claws on its hind feet which it can use to inflict deep scratches on anything holding it, and several of the larger frogs and toads also kick powerfully if restrained.

Parasites

Less obvious than predators but equally important to frogs' survival are parasites. It seems that every species is a potential host to a wide range of these organisms, some of which confine themselves to a single species or group of species, and some of which are more catholic in their choice. The unwritten rule amongst efficient parasites is to avoid killing the host – this would be a short-cut to extinction – but a heavy parasite burden is still bad news for the frog since it may weaken it and make it less able to survive the many other hazards of life. Although a huge array of frog parasites have been catalogued, and their life-cycles worked out, their effect on frog populations, and the frogs' defence against them, are largely unknown. It would be tedious to list all of the known parasites of frogs, but a few of the more important and interesting ones are worth noting.

Protozoan parasites

Protozoans (i.e. single-celled animals) which parasitise frogs include *Plasmodium bufonis*, the so-called 'amphibian malaria' which is transmitted by mosquitoes, but by far the best documented species are the *Opalina* species, especially *O. ranarum*. This organism is often present in every single individual of a population of frogs, although it probably has little effect on their health. When the host is in its terrestrial, non-breeding phase only 'adult' *Opalina* are found in the frog's gut, but about fourteen days before breeding is due to start these begin to divide and give rise to numerous cysts which are released into the water as soon as the breeding frogs enter it. If these cysts are ingested by a tadpole they may divide again and complete a second generation in that season, or they may remain in its gut and develop into adult organisms, there to stay until the frog becomes sexually mature and goes into the water to breed. The interesting thing about this life-cycle, therefore, is that it is geared to the frog's reproductive cycle – the *Opalina* begins to divide when it detects reproductive hormones in the frog's system.

Helminths (worms and flukes)

Many species of worms and flukes are associated with frogs – their incidence may be as high as 50 per cent of the animals in a population. *Polystoma interrimum* is common in North American and European species. It produces eggs when the frog goes into the water to breed and these are excreted. The eggs are synchronised to hatch at the time that the tadpole reaches the internal gill stage and the larval parasite, which is barrel-shaped with a sucker bearing sixteen hooks, enters the branchial pore of the tadpole and attaches itself to the gill. Here it feeds on mucus and detritus until it matures into a juvenile worm. At this stage it leaves the gill and migrates over the surface of the tadpole to enter its cloaca. If this seems a chancy system, the fluke which infests *Scaphiopus bombifrons* is even more remarkable. It lives in the bladder of these frogs and due to their explosive and irregular breeding habits it must be equally opportunistic in spreading amongst the population. As soon as the toads burrow upwards and enter the temporary pools in which they breed, large numbers of larval flukes leave the toads' bladders and swim around until they find new hosts. They then crawl over the skin and enter via the nostrils and from here they make their way to the lungs, where they mature. Only then do they migrate through the animals' bodies to take up residence in the bladder and await the next breeding season.

Some of the higher orders of parasites have stages in their life-cycles which infest different animals. Many of these are quite complicated, for example, the *Haematoloechus* flukes, which are common in the lungs of *Rana* and *Bufo* species, become adult in the frogs and lay eggs which are excreted into the water. These are eaten by water snails and hatch, bore out of the snail and become free-living 'cercaria'. These then penetrate a larval insect such as a dragonfly nymph, and encyst. The insect eventually metamorphoses into an adult insect and, if it is eaten by a frog, the life-cycle can begin again. A related species, *Opisthoglyphe ranae*, skips the insect stage and enters a tadpole instead. It then relies on the tadpole being eaten by a frog – this tells us quite a lot about the frequency with which frogs prey on tadpoles.

The eggs of frogs which are laid out of water, e.g. on overhanging

Plate 29   *Rhacophorus bimaculatus*, an Asian tree frog, with a leech attached to its back leg. Terrestrial leeches are especially common in South East Asia but their effect on frogs is probably minimal.

vegetation, in foam nests or on damp ground, or eggs which form clumps on the surface, are prone to parasitism by fly larvae (maggots). For instance, a drosophilid fly lays its eggs near the egg-masses of *Centrolenella fleischmanni*, which are laid on leaves overhanging streams. The maggots feed on the embryos and complete their life-cycle 10–13 days later. Other *Centrolenella* species, in which the male stays near the eggs after they have been laid, are not so likely to be attacked in this way and so the presence of the male presumably prevents the flies from laying their eggs. Parasitism of eggs by fly larvae is also reported for *Hyla* and *Nyctimystes* species from New Guinea, for the leptodactylid *Physalaemus pustulosus* and the rhacophorid *Polypedates leucomystax*, the latter two species being foam-nest builders from South America and South East Asia respectively.

Ecto-parasites

The most important ecto-parasites of frogs are leeches. These are common in South East Asia and may occasionally be found attached to frogs (plate 29). They live on the host only temporarily and drop off when they have fed. Their impact on the health of the frog is unknown.

This section has mentioned just a few of the thousands of parasites which infest frogs. We know very little about the frogs' resistance or defence against them, only that no frogs seem to be immune and that some populations exist with 100 per cent parasite infestation. In view of the fact that most parasites spread throughout populations when they enter water to breed, it would be especially interesting to know if terrestrial breeding in frogs leads to a reduction in parasite load.

Chapter 5
Food and Feeding

In their adult stage, all frogs and toads are carnivorous. A few species, notably *Bufo marinus*, are also known to consume a certain amount of vegetable matter but this must be regarded as the exception to the rule. Furthermore, nearly all species appear to be stimulated to feed by movement, therefore their prey must normally be living (again, *Bufo marinus* is an exception because it will take carrion, as well as dog food, etc.). Due to their size, most frogs and toads are limited to a diet of small invertebrates – ants, termites, beetles, slugs, snails, earthworms and so on – the main factor being availability rather than any great degree of selection on the part of the frog although a few species do seem to specialise to some extent. Some of the larger species are more ambitious and eat small vertebrates – rodents, fledgling birds, young snakes, other species of frogs and toads, and, on occasion, smaller members of their own species. Since all frogs must swallow their food whole, its size is

Plate 30   The wide gape of this young African bullfrog enables it to tackle proportionately large prey, especially other frogs.

strictly limited by the width of their mouth, and some of the more voracious species – *Ceratophrys* species are good examples – can successfully tackle prey which would appear to be much too large for them. Two species from the mountains of Ethiopia, *Tornierella obscura* and *T. kouniensis*, are specialised mollusc eaters. As well as slugs, these frogs, measuring up to 50 mm, feed on land snails up to 5 × 8 mm in size, and swallow the whole animal, shell and all, their skulls being specially modified to allow for this. Amongst the more remarkable prey items recorded, the American bullfrog, *Rana catesbeiana*, has been observed eating bats on more than one occasion, but the prize must surely go to the African bullfrog, *Pyxicephalus adspersus*, which was found in a snake enclosure at Pretoria zoo having eaten sixteen complete young ringhals cobras, *Haemachatus hemachatus*, as well as the front half of a seventeenth[1]

Aquatic species take fish, which they catch and swallow underwater, although the smaller kinds are limited to aquatic invertebrates such as insect larvae and crustaceans. *Discodeles guppyi* from the Solomon Islands occasionally eats land crabs and the large Asian species *Rana crancivora* is known as the crab-eating frog but lives up to its name only where it occurs in brackish swamps and, even here, it is doubtful if these seemingly unpalatable items make up more than a part of its diet. Many semi-aquatic species, such as the fire-bellied toads, *Bombina*, and many ranids, are adept at catching flying insects which land on the water's surface or fly just above it.

Hunting strategy

Techniques for finding food are varied and often reflect the habits of the preferred prey of the species in question. For instance, those species which feed primarily on termites, visit, or sometimes live permanently in, the galleries which these insects inhabit. In general though, frogs and toads are opportunistic feeders and tackle most moving prey if it fits into the appropriate size range. During the day, many species remain hidden beneath the ground, under rocks, etc., and in these situations potential prey may conveniently wander by, in which case it will probably be snapped up. At night, nocturnal species often roam about randomly, encountering a variety of the small invertebrates which are abundant in damp and overgrown places. At other times they may actively forage in places where prey is likely to congregate and it is not uncommon to find a gathering of toads such as *Bufo marinus* (in areas where this species occurs) sitting in a circle at the edge of the pool of light cast by a street or garden light, picking off flying insects such as cockroaches and moths which are attracted in large numbers. The European common toad, *Bufo bufo*, has been observed sitting by the entrance to a bee-hive in the early evening, intercepting the bees as they return from their pollen-gathering activities.

Other species ambush their prey by hiding in likely places. Many of these species are cryptically marked, for example the Asian horned toad, *Megophrys nasuta* (plate 22) and its South American counterpart, the

Plate 31 'Sit and wait' tactics call for good camouflage. This *Ceratophrys calcarata* has partially buried itself in order to ambush its prey.

Ceratophrys species (plate 31), and these animals wait, half buried in leaf-litter until suitable prey blunders by. All of these species, and other similar examples, eat large and wary prey such as rodents and smaller frogs – it may be that the more cunning 'sit and wait' tactics are far more effective against this type of prey, or perhaps smaller species carry out the same behaviour but, being less conspicuous, have not been observed so carefully. Certainly, these larger species are more sluggish and ungainly than their quicker and more agile relatives, many of which are able to launch themselves at flying insects and catch them in full flight.

When prey is located, be it an ant, beetle or mouse, it is usually studied for a few seconds and the frog may raise the front part of its body to give an improved angle of attack. (It may also twitch its toes, much as a stalking cat twitches its tail – it is not known if this action serves any useful purpose but it has been suggested that the movement may lure the prey to within striking distance.) If the prey stops moving, the frog waits. After a while it may lose interest but at the slightest hint of movement – the flickering of an antenna or the re-arrangement of a limb – the frog reacts. The way in which it reacts depends on the structure of its tongue; in most species this is attached at the front of the mouth, not the back, and it can be flicked out and, because it is liberally coated with mucus, the prey sticks to it as though it were fly-paper, and is drawn into the mouth (fig. 9). Some species, e.g. the fire-bellied toads and other members of their family (Discoglossidae), have a different type of tongue which cannot be extended out of the mouth and so these use a less sophisticated means of capturing prey – they simply lunge forward and grab it in their mouth, sometimes using their forearms and hands to cram it in or to prevent its escape.

Fig. 9 Prey capture in many species is accomplished by flipping out a sticky tongue. This is attached at the front of the mouth and points backwards when withdrawn.

Aquatic frogs of the family Pipidae, e.g. the Surinam toad, *Pipa pipa*, and the African clawed frogs, *Xenopus* species, do not have tongues at all and rely heavily on their hands to assist in making a capture. They habitually sit motionless in the water with their arms and fingers out-stretched: the finger-tips seem unusually sensitive both to touch and to any movement in the water, such as that caused by another animal swimming close by. As soon as they sense anything within range they instantly scoop it towards their mouth with their front limbs, at the same time moving quickly forward with a single thrust of their powerful hind limbs. If the 'prey' is edible and of a suitable size it is grasped in the mouth and, in the case of a large meal, the hands are used like a pair of dining forks to manipulate it into a position which is convenient for swallowing.

Because the feeding reflex is so strong, frogs will often attempt to eat prey which is unpalatable or distasteful. It may be spat out or regurgitated later and it seems as though after a few of these experiences unsuitable prey is rejected on sight. Many such organisms are distinctively coloured in combinations of black and yellow, white or red (in much the same way as frogs which are poisonous are so coloured).

Swallowing and digestion

Having considered the techniques of feeding, we should also look at the equipment with which frogs catch, swallow and digest their food. The frog's teeth are similar in structure to those of other vertebrates, but their arrangement is slightly unusual. Species belonging to the genera *Pipa* and *Bufo* lack teeth altogether. Most other species have teeth on the upper jaw only, but may have additional rows of teeth on the roof of their mouth (vomerine teeth). Of the species which do have teeth on the lower jaw (a few ranids and hylids), in one, *Petropedates natator*, a West African ranid, these are present only in the male. Most species, while lacking true teeth on one or both jaws, have notches or serrations formed from the jaw itself and these obviously serve to grasp prey. A few species, such as the Australian *Adelotus brevis*, have 'false tusks' at the front of the lower jaw which can apparently also be used defensively.

Swallowing, especially in those terrestrial species which eat relatively large prey, often appears to be a somewhat uncomfortable operation. Two or three gulps are usually followed by the retraction of the eyeballs into the skull, sometimes one at a time, sometimes both together, as they are pressed down into the buccal cavity where they help to force the food down the frog's throat. This is made possible by the flexible nature of the roof of the mouth and by the tough protective casing in which the eyeball rests.

As the food makes its way down towards the stomach, an enzyme, pepsin, may be secreted in the oesophagus to begin the digestive process. This continues with the addition of various other secretions within the stomach itself, before the partly digested food passes into the coiled large and small intestines, and eventually to the cloaca, a common opening for the urinary, digestive and reproductive tracts.

In contrast to the carnivorous habits of adult frogs and toads, most tadpoles are semi-herbivorous, feeding largely on algae and bacteria. Tadpoles of the more primitive species, e.g. *Xenopus* species and the species of *Pipa* which have free-swimming larvae, obtain their food by filtering

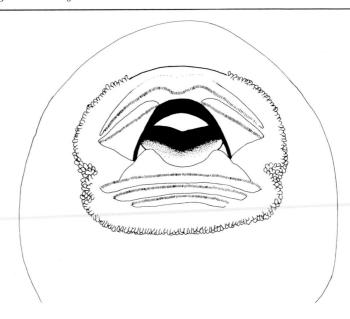

Fig. 10   Mouthparts of a typical tadpole. Rows of rasping cusps are arranged around a central beak-like mouth.

suspended particles from the water. They achieve this by holding themselves in a characteristic 'head-down' posture in mid-water and taking regular gulps. To improve the efficiency of this method they beat their long filament-like tails continually to create a flow of water and food (a kind of organic soup) towards their mouths. As the water enters the buccal cavity it is pumped back towards the gill chamber, but first passes through a filtration mechanism which traps the suspended particles. These then swirl about until they come into contact with a patch of sticky cells which entangles them and transports them to the entrance of the digestive tract, the oesophagus. In this way, particles measuring anything from 0.2μ upwards are consumed, almost as a by-product of the respiratory process, as the filtered water continues into the gill chambers, where the oxygen is removed.

Tadpoles of species which are more advanced than *Xenopus* and its relatives, i.e. the majority of species, have an additional refinement in the form of a series of horny rasps arranged around the mouth, with which they scrape food particles from the substrate, avoiding the necessity of living in organically rich water (fig. 10). These species typically feed by grazing on the layer of algae and bacteria which grows on leaves, rocks and detritus, although they also take food from the surface film by swimming upside down, and sometimes use their jaws to chop small fragments from soft or decaying plants. The particles of food so gathered are then swallowed and filtered using the same method as described for the filter-feeders. Some species seem to alternate between these methods of feeding, and graze or filter food according to the conditions. A few species feed only from the surface and do so more efficiently when their mouths are positioned on the top of their head, surrounded by a funnel-shaped structure, as in some *Megophrys* and *Phyllomedusa* species. Because plant material is not easily digested, a long gut is necessary to allow the various digestive secretions time to work. The tadpole's gut is therefore spirally coiled and takes up most of the space within its abdomen, where it is often clearly visible through the body wall.

Most of the grazers will vary their diet by scraping cells from dead animals if these happen to be present, but a few species are predatory, such as the tadpoles of *Hymenochirus boettgeri*, which feed on small aquatic arthropods, and those of *Ceratophrys* species, which have specialised mouthparts. The situation in some of the American spadefoot toads, *Scaphiopus*, is rather more complex. Some tadpoles have the mouthparts of a typical grazer, whereas others develop powerful jaw muscles and a notched beak. These latter types prey not only on the tadpoles of other frogs, e.g. *Bufo cognatus*, but also on members of their own species, usually the herbivorous form, which tend to be smaller. It seems that the species' specialised breeding sites, consisting of temporary pools, has resulted in the evolution of a kind of insurance policy whereby some individuals can grow quickly, at the expense of the others, and so gain a better chance of metamorphosing should the pools dry up quickly – in good years the grazers probably have an advantage because their mouth is heavily muscled and it sucks the eggs in whole, while the gut is unlimited. The predatory kind comes into its own when pools begin to dry out, thus concentrating the remaining tadpoles into small puddles where they are easily caught and devoured.

Some tadpoles specialise in eating frogs' eggs. *Anotheca coronatum*, a hylid from Central America, spends its larval life in the vases of bromeliad plants where it appears to eat only the eggs of other frogs (possibly including its own species, although this has not been definitely established) which come along to spawn later. The region around its mouth is heavily muscled and it sucks the eggs in whole, while the gut is shorter and much less coiled that that of typical, herbivorous, tadpoles. *Hyla zeteki* tadpoles are similar in habits – they too live in bromeliad vases and eat only frogs' eggs – and in Asia (where there are no bromeliad plants) a rhacophorid, *Philautus* species (possibly *P. carinensis*) lays its eggs in water-filled tree-holes which are devoid of nutrient – the tadpoles are known to eat frogs' eggs but there appear to be no other arboreal species in the region. It seems as though they must feed entirely on eggs of their own species, and it has been suggested that females purposely lay infertile eggs for the benefit of their developing tadpoles. This rather surprising theory is not unprecedented – three species of dendrobatid frogs, *Dendrobates histrionicus*, *lehmanni* and *pumilio*, are known to do just this. They carry their tadpoles one or two at a time to bromeliad vases within a well-defined territory. The female visits each bromeliad in turn every few days and lays a single, highly nourishing 'food egg' in the vase, on which the growing tadpole feeds. As far as is known, these are the only examples amongst the amphibians of a parent directly providing food for its offspring.

It should be mentioned that the tadpoles of quite a large number of species do not feed at all. Instead, the egg contains sufficient yolk to nourish them until they metamorphose. In this way they can live in small bodies of water, such as those in tree-holes and small depressions in the ground, which would not otherwise be suitable, and these are usually free from predators. A varied selection of species exploits this system: several ranids, microhylids and a bufonid from Africa and Madagascar; some of the South American leptodactylids; and the Australian myobatrachids belonging to the genus *Kyarranus*.

Non-feeding tadpoles of the marsupial frogs *Flectonotus* and *Fritziana* begin their development in a pouch on their mother's back and complete it in bromeliad vases, and tadpoles of *Sooglossus seychellensis*, *Assa darlingtoni*, *Rheobatrachus silus* and *R. vitellinus* are carried until metamorphosis and are therefore presumably unable to feed. On the other hand, it has been suggested that the tadpoles of Darwin's frog, *Rhinoderma darwini*, which develop in the vocal pouch of the male, *do* feed – on substances which he secretes inside the pouch.

Chapter 6
Reproduction 1 – the mating game

To most European and North American naturalists the sequence of events which forms the reproductive cycle of frogs and toads is pretty well known and straightforward: the adult animals come into breeding condition, usually in the spring, migrate to ponds and ditches where they pair up in a position known as amplexus and as the female lays her clumps or strings of spawn the male releases his sperm simultaneously to fertilise them. After the adults have left the water the eggs hatch into tadpoles, eventually grow legs, lose their tails and emerge from the water to disperse across the surrounding countryside.

This is a very simplified account of what is in fact an astonishing aspect of biology. Each stage in the cycle is prone to variation and a surprisingly large number of species, perhaps as many as half of those known, depart completely from 'conventional' reproductive activities and do something entirely different. It is not an exaggeration to say that in their manner of reproduction, frogs are the most diverse vertebrates on earth. Fertilisation may be internal or external, the eggs may be laid in or out of the water, the tadpoles may or may not feed or there may not be any tadpoles at all and, finally, a few species give birth to living young. Superimposed on this diversity is the variation in their habitats and factors such as competition and predation which have given rise to so many different life-histories, making a study of them both stimulating and, at times, confusing.

This chapter will deal with the general principles of reproductive strategy, and the following two will go on to describe the development of frogs and toads, and then some typical and not-so-typical life-histories.

Pre-mating activities

Before spawning can take place the adult frogs must be in a state of reproductive readiness, which is achieved by feeding well and producing the male and female sex cells – eggs, or ova, in the case of females, and sperm in the case of males. Production of these cells is initiated by hormones from the pituitary gland (see Chapter 3), which is in turn stimulated by a variety of environmental factors, amongst which are rainfall, and increasing or decreasing daylength and temperature (in species from temperate regions). The exact values of these parameters will vary according to the species' range, and with widespread species there may even be differences between populations. For instance, males of the European common toad, *Bufo bufo*, become sexually active (i.e.

Plate 32   *Hyla boans*, a giant tree frog, calling near a small river in Trinidad: the vocal pouch is greatly extended.

they begin to call) at lower temperatures (about 3.5°C) in the north of England than they do in the south (at about 7.5°C). Other environmental cues may include the gradually increasing atmospheric pressure which precedes a period of rain, or the appearance of a food item of seasonal availability – this aspect is one about which we seem to know very little, and it is quite likely that some species are stimulated by factors which we have not even dreamt of.

Breeding seasons

Species which breed at roughly the same time every year are said to be cyclic breeders: their ovaries or testes follow a predictable annual pattern of cellular activity. The European common frog is an example: it enters hibernation with eggs or sperm partially or completely formed so that it is ready to breed as soon as it becomes active again in the spring. This gives the tadpoles the maximum length of time in which to complete their development, an important requirement for species from regions with cold winters or a period of dry weather.

In places where conditions are suitable for breeding over most or all of the year, at least some animals will be reproductively 'ripe' at any given time and the breeding season will be extended. This condition is found in most tropical frogs, which begin to breed at the onset of the rainy season and continue right through until the dry season begins (often as long as nine or ten months). During this period, males call every night but each female visits them only when her eggs are ready to be laid – under laboratory conditions this may be every ten days but, unfortunately, few thorough field studies have been carried out to see if this potential is realised under natural conditions. Much research is needed in this area.

Somewhere between these two extremes are a relatively small number of species which are opportunists: they spend much of their time beneath the surface in dry regions of North America, Australia and Africa, always in a state of reproductive readiness should the time come. As soon as the first few drops of rain hit the surface, they burrow out and spawn within hours to take advantage of the surface water, which may not remain for very long. Often their eggs come to nothing as the pools dry up before their tadpoles have metamorphosed, but by repeating the performance every time there is heavy rain, sooner or later another generation will survive.

Broadly speaking, then, there are three categories of breeding:

  (i) those frogs which spawn simultaneously at roughly the same time every year (seasonal or cyclic breeders)
  (ii) those which spawn simultaneously whenever suitable conditions come along (opportunistic breeders)

(iii) those which extend their breeding over a prolonged period or even throughout the year (continuous breeders)

The call

Frogs were the first animals to evolve a true voice (the sounds produced by insects are the results of mechanical actions – one part of the body being rubbed or scraped on another). In frogs, the call is produced by the movement of air across a series of vocal cords. Preparatory to calling the frog fills its lungs with air and then closes its mouth and nostrils. The air is then moved forwards, inflating the vocal pouch, or vocal sac – a single or paired balloon-like structure formed from the floor of its mouth (fig. 11). By moving air back and forth from body to pouch, and so over the vocal cords, a variety of sounds can be produced: whistles, trills, croaks, grunts, chuckles, pops and warbles, depending on species. Various calls have been likened to blowing across the top of an empty bottle, running a finger along the teeth of a comb, or moving a squeaky

Fig. 11   Variation in the position and shape of vocal sacs: paired, bi-lobed and single.

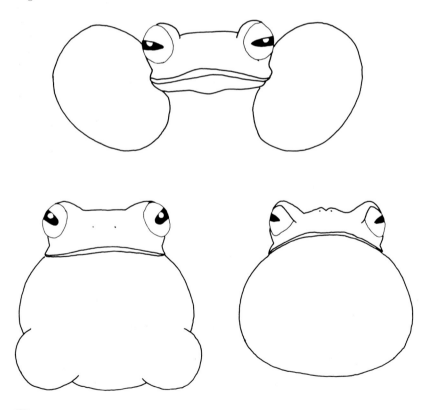

wheelbarrow about, and several species have earned themselves popular names which allude to the sound of their call: bullfrog, sheep frog, barking tree frog, spring peeper, tinsmith, etc.

Generally speaking, small frogs have high-pitched calls and large frogs have low-pitched calls – this applies to different species as well as to small and large individuals, but some species make calls which do not follow this rule. For instance, burrowing frogs, which call from beneath the surface, e.g. many microhylids, have low frequency (< 1kHz) calls so that these will penetrate the substrate, whereas species which live alongside fast-flowing streams and waterfalls often have high-pitched chirping calls in order to be heard above the sound of the water.

Frog calls are often thought of as straightforward 'come and find me' invitations to females, but it is now recognised that calling males may be putting across up to three messages at the same time.

Species isolation

One important aspect of frogs' calls is that each species has a unique 'tune' to which only members of the same species will react. This is of great importance where several species occur together – it eliminates the problem of females mating with males of the wrong species and so wasting their eggs (which may have taken several months to produce) on a sterile mating. The call therefore isolates one species from another and is known as a 'pre-mating isolating mechanism'. It is interesting to note that if two similar species have ranges which overlap in one place, their calls will be more distinct here than in areas where only one occurs – their differences are emphasised where it matters the most. A spin-off of this arrangement is that scientists are able to identify similar frogs accurately by recording and analysing their calls. This recent observation has been made possible by modern techniques of recording the frogs' calls and then turning the sounds into 'pictures' known as sonograms and comparing them with one another – the traditional method of classifying frogs from pickled museum specimens, though still having its uses, can no longer be relied upon completely. This 'auditory fingerprinting' has led to the discovery that several populations of frogs which were formerly considered to belong to a single species are now known to consist of two – outwardly they may be difficult or impossible to distinguish but since differing calls effectively give rise to separate breeding populations these must, by definition, be separate species. A well-known example concerns the North American grey tree frogs, formerly all known as *Hyla versicolor*, but now divided into two species, *H. versicolor* and *H. chrysoscelis*, on the basis of two distinct types of call (although they can also be distinguished, with difficulty, by other means).

Some species do not share their habitats with other frogs, so why do these call? In some cases, they do not. Quite a few species which are isolated by virtue of where they live or their breeding season, etc., and in which the problem of hybridisation would not occur, are mute. Examples are: most species of *Atelopus*, *Bufo superciliaris* and *Ascaphus truei*. It

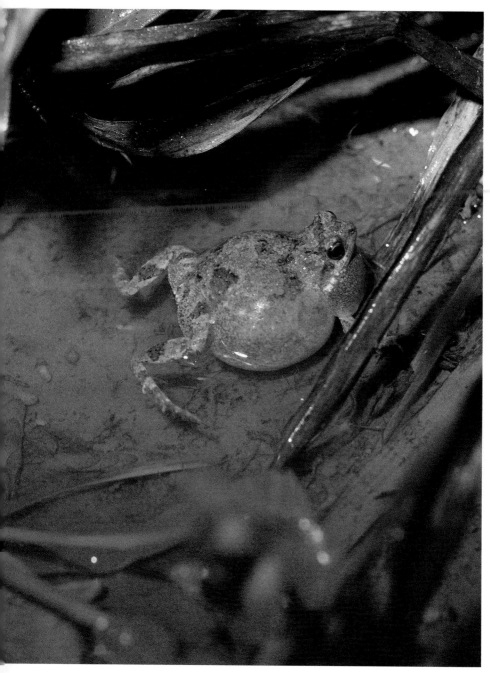

Plate 33 *Physalaemus pustulosus* calling from a shallow puddle. Here, the body is inflated, prior to shunting air across the vocal cords and into the vocal pouch.

74

Plate 34 A confrontation between two male *Hyla granosa*. One has encroached on the other's territory and will be rebuffed with loud and frequent calls.

Plate 35 Two male *Phyllomedusa trinitatus* 'wrestling' for the right to call in a territory, in this case part of a bush overhanging a small pool.

must also be borne in mind that calling can attract predators and there is therefore a trade-off between being a successful father and a tasty morsel!

Territoriality

In most frogs, possession of a territory is a prerequisite for obtaining a mate. The better the territory, the higher the chances of attracting a female. The quality of a territory may depend on its size, its suitability for egg-laying, or other factors, but male frogs go to great lengths to define and defend their 'patch'. The call is therefore also used as an advertisement to other males, letting them know that the territory is occupied. If another male encroaches, the territory holder will face the intruder and may move towards him (plate 34), at the same time increasing his call rate or changing to a completely different 'tune', known as an 'encounter call'. Usually this is sufficient to force the intruder away or at least to remain silent, but sometimes such an encounter ends in physical conflict, with the frogs grappling and even biting each other to settle the dispute. (The tusks and spines which can be found on the males of some species, e.g. *Adelotus brevis*, *Leptobrachium boringii*, and *Centrolenella* species, are used for this purpose and have been known to inflict serious, sometimes fatal, injuries.)

The size of the territory will depend on the species concerned; some males call in dense aggregations in which each territory is only a few square centimetres, whereas others insist on many square metres – it all depends on the breeding system (see below), the availability of suitable spawning sites and the density of the population.

Mate attraction

Quite a few species spawn in tree-holes, bromeliad vases, underground burrows or chambers, or beneath logs, etc., and here the male's call is necessary to direct the female. Of the species which form choruses, in some cases these may also help to guide the females to the spawning site. This may be especially important for species which breed in temporary pools and puddles which may not always be in the same place from one breeding season to another, but each male is only really interested in attracting a female to himself, not to a whole group of his rivals, so how does he go about this?

It has been found experimentally that a female will move towards the call which is loudest, goes on for longest, or which is the most elaborate (or a combination of all three). It has also been shown that it is the biggest males which make these calls and that smaller males keep their distance from these males (in response to the calls). So the males which call best end up with the most females, even though the initial effect is to establish a territory. Occasionally a frog will make a call consisting of two components, one of which attracts females and has no effect on nearby males and the other of which has the opposite effect.

From these observations it is obvious that there is an interplay between calling to establish a territory and calling to attract a mate.

Mention should be made of an alternative method of communication, although its significance is not yet fully understood. Blue-footed frogs, *Staurois natator*, from Borneo (plate 95), live close to torrents and waterfalls, the sound of which tends to mask animal vocalisations. The males of this species go through a stereotyped 'semaphore' display in which a hind leg is raised and held at right angles to the body at the same time as the toes are spread widely in order to reveal the bright blue webbing between them. This is repeated several times, occasionally with alternating feet. Although the obvious conclusion is that this behaviour serves to attract a mate, instead of a call which could not be heard very well, there is no clear evidence that this takes place. In fact, *Staurois* does have a voice, a high-pitched, bird-like trill, but it tends to use this when it is alarmed.

Breeding systems

The breeding system of a species or population of frogs is the product of its seasonal pattern, its calling behaviour, and the density of animals at the breeding site.

Species in which all of the population breed at the same time in dense aggregations are said to be 'explosive' breeders. Examples are the European common toads, *Bufo bufo* (cyclic breeders), and the North American spadefoot toads, *Scaphiopus* species (opportunists). There is rarely any subtlety in their mate selection – the males often arrive at the ponds just before the females and congregate in a favourable area with little or no obvious territorial behaviour. As the females arrive and enter the water, the males mill around, grasping anything of approximately the right size – a piece of wood, a human hand, another male or, occasionally, a ripe female. When this happens the male retains his grip and is carried about by the female. At this point other males may get involved, trying to force their way between the male and female, and he will probably respond by kicking them away with one of his hind feet. If he is a small male it is likely that he will eventually be ousted by a larger one, and this often happens to small males who try to beat the system by ambushing a female before she reaches the pond and entering it while in amplexus – large males rarely do this, obviously being in a better position to find a mate even if she is already 'occupied'. Eventually the female will spawn and leave the pond, but the male will return to the 'pool' of other males in the hope of finding another mate. After three or four nights the supply of females will have dried up and the males too will disperse.

The situation with species that have extended breeding seasons (i.e. the majority) is far more complex. Males of these species always call. It is not known if all the males in one area call every night, or even if they return to the same place to call, but they invariably space themselves out fairly evenly and may fight or display to each other if their territory is encroached upon (see above). In all the species which have been studied

Plate 36   A pair of European common frogs add their spawn to that of numerous other pairs which have bred within a day or two of each other.

so far, males do not actively search for females but rely on their call to attract them. Only when a female approaches or touches a male does he attempt amplexus. Since the spawning period is prolonged, only a small proportion of the local females will spawn on any given night and it seems likely that a particularly 'attractive' male may be involved in a high percentage of possible matings spread over several nights while others never mate at all.

The usual pattern of calling in species which form choruses is for one male to start calling and the others to join in. The number of calls builds up to a crescendo and then gradually peters out, the whole process being repeated a few minutes later. It appears that the same male usually initiates calling and is also the last to stop: he is known as the bout leader and is often more successful than other males in obtaining mates. The other males continue calling because sooner or later the bout leader

Plate 37   Axillary amplexus, demonstrated by a pair of *Phyllomedusa trinitatus*.

will find a mate and then it will be the turn of one of them to become the bout leader. It may also be that, by calling together, the frogs are interfering with each others' calls and so reducing the advantage of the bout leader over them.

Where the density of males is low, calling stations are usually well spaced out, often several metres apart. Under these circumstances, males often do not form choruses but call alternately so that there is little or no overlap – an observer listening to these calls often gets the impression that one male is 'answering' another but it is more likely that each is trying to avoid synchronous calling so that he can be heard clearly. How do females select males when this happens? Obviously, the male which is calling nearest will appear to have the loudest voice, and so an alternative means of assessing male vigour seems likely. Although research is by no means conclusive, it seems that in this type of situation the female favours the male with the deepest voice, irrespective of volume, and since the biggest males make the deepest croaks, these are the most successful.

As in most aspects of life, some individuals just do not stick to the rules. If a frog only has a small voice he may 'realise' that he is unlikely to attract females on his own merit and so, rather than competing openly, he may creep into the territory of a vigorous caller with the intention of intercepting females headed in his direction. In some breeding populations each calling male is surrounded by these 'satellite' males and, although it seems that their strategy is rarely successful, the slender possibility of stealing a mate in this way is their only hope. It could be that the structure of the population is important. If there are far more males than females (on a given night) the chances of the weak-voiced males getting one will be so slight that 'poaching' one from a bigger male will be the most sensible thing to do, but if there is not such a surplus of males then it will be more worthwhile to call even for small individuals – not all of the females can mate with the biggest male(s). Although the males cannot assess how many females are likely to come to the pond, thousands of generations will have favoured whichever system is the most effective for a given species under given circumstances.

Taking breeding systems as a whole, whichever one is at work, two basic strategies can be recognised: in species which breed explosively, males fight amongst themselves for females (direct male-male competition); but, in species with extended or prolonged breeding seasons, mate choice is left to the females and male-male competition, if it exists at all, is limited to the right to call and the possession of a territory. It should be noted that these are the two extremes, between which are systems containing some of each strategy – even within the same population, the density of calling males may change in the course of a single night and at some point the males switch from attracting females to a general free-for-all and vice versa.

It should be remembered that much of what is known about frogs' breeding strategies comes from a small number of studies on miscellaneous species. This makes it difficult to generalise and it will be a long time before the complete story is fully understood.

Amplexus

Having found, or been found by, a mate, the male takes up a position in which he can fertilise the eggs. With a few exceptions, this occurs outside the female's body, immediately after the eggs have been expelled and before the jelly surrounding them swells. In order to ensure that his sperm comes into contact with as many of them as possible it is important that he positions his cloaca as close to hers as possible. This position is known as amplexus and there are two main types and a number of variations:

Inguinal amplexus

The males of six families of primitive frogs (Leiopelmatidae, Discoglossidae, Pipidae, Rhinophrynidae, Pelobatidae and Pelodytidae) and the males of some species belonging to two of the more advanced families (Myobatrachidae and Leptodactylidae) grasp the females just in front of the hind limbs. During egg-laying they bend their bodies so that the cloaca is in close proximity to that of the female.

Axillary amplexus

Males of all the other, more advanced, families (apart from those listed elsewhere) grasp the female immediately behind the fore-limbs. In this way their cloacae are close to each other without any special manoeuvres being necessary on the part of the male.

Cephalic amplexus

Some frogs of the Dendrobatidae (poison dart frogs), all of which lay their eggs on land, take up a position in which the male presses the outside, i.e. the back, of his hands against the female's chin or throat. This position has been observed in at least one species from each of the main dendrobatid genera, *Colostethus inguinalis*, *Dendrobates tricolor*, and *Phyllobates terribilis*.

Straddle amplexus

An unusual form of amplexus occurs in at least three species of ranids from Madagascar, all belonging to the genus *Mantidactylus*, in which the male does not grasp the female, but in which she forces her head beneath his hind legs while he is clinging to a vertical leaf. Since this always occurs during rain, it is assumed that the sperm is released onto the back of the female and flows down over the eggs as they are laid.

Glued amplexus

Some frogs are so rotund and have such short limbs that any form of conventional amplexus would be a physical impossibility. In these species the male secretes a sticky substance from glands in his abdominal region and attaches himself with this to the back of the female. Species in which this has been confirmed are those belonging to the microhylid genera *Kaloula*, *Gastrophryne* and *Breviceps*, but it is also suspected in other similarly shaped species. The attachment is said to be so effective that any attempt to separate the frogs would result in damage. After egg-laying, the substance breaks down or the female sheds her skin, and the animals are free to go their separate ways.

Prolonged amplexus

Whereas in most frogs amplexus lasts for a few hours at most, some species stay coupled for several days or even weeks. Frogs of the genus *Atelopus* are especially prone to this arrangement. Males of *A. oxyrhynchus* and *A. ignescens* have been observed in amplexus over a period of several months, the females continuing to feed as usual but the males, unable to feed efficiently if at all, becoming thinner and thinner. It is not known

Fig. 12   The unique 'tail' of male *Ascaphus truei* is used to transfer sperm directly into the cloaca of the female. This is the only known example of internal fertilisation in an aquatic-breeding frog, although it occurs in several terrestrial breeding species.

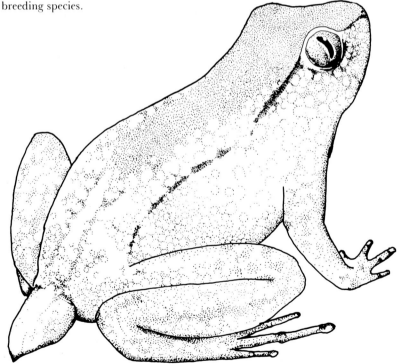

Plate 38   Love or war? Ritualised amplexus is common to courting couples and to fighting males in many dendrobatids. This is *Phyllobates bicolor*: since both sexes are similar in appearance, this encounter could be either type of interaction.

what the advantages of this system are, although because *Atelopus* live in widespread populations on high altitude moorland it may be that the males grab females whenever possible and hang on until breeding time – *A. ignescens* migrates over long distances and in huge numbers to get to its breeding sites and, invariably, each female is already partnered by the time she arrives.

Internal fertilisation

In a radical departure from conventional frog reproduction, a few species fertilise the eggs before they are laid. These are: five species of *Nectophry-noides* from Africa (Bufonidae); *Ascaphus truei* from North America (Leiopelmatidae), *Eleutherodactylus jasperi* and *E. coqui* from Puerto Rico

83

and *E. angelicus* from Costa Rica (Leptodactylidae). In addition, internal fertilisation is suspected in the small bufonid *Mertensophryne micranotis* from Kenya: the males have a ring of small spines around their cloaca and these are thought to maintain it in the correct position while sperm is transferred to the female – unfortunately, it breeds in holes and crevices about 1.5 metres up in rotten tree-trunks and so it is difficult to be sure. In *Ascaphus* and *Eleutherodactylus* internal fertilisation is accomplished after a period of conventional amplexus – inguinal in *Ascaphus*, axillary in *Eleutherodactylus* – and *Ascaphus* has an additional refinement in the form of a short intromittent organ, the 'tail', which gives it its common name of tailed frog. In at least two of the *Nectophrynoides* species, *N. malcomi* and *N. occidentalis*, amplexus is inguinal but ventral – apparently, in *N. malcomi* several males cling to a female but only the successful male is upside down. In *Mertensophryne micranotis* amplexus lasts for up to ten hours, with the eggs being laid some time later.

Token or cursory amplexus

Species which lay eggs on the land are not faced with the problem of loss of sperm as is the case with aquatic species. Although many of them still retain one or other of the above types of amplexus, others employ only a brief, ritualised amplexus, probably as a means of stimulating egg-laying, the actual fertilisation being achieved in other ways. This 'token' amplexus has been noted in Darwin's frog, *Rhinoderma darwini*, in several dendrobatids, for instance *Dendrobates pumilio* and *D. granulifera*, and some of the Madagascan ranids, such as the golden mantella, *Mantella aurantiaca*.

Secondary sex characteristics

Apart from their reproductive systems, other differences exist between male and female frogs, either permanently or during the breeding season. These are known as secondary sex characteristics, and include the presence of vocal sacs in males (see above). Others are described here.

As anyone who has tried to grasp a wet and slippery frog will know, the male's task of maintaining an amplectic grip for any length of time is not an easy one. In order to facilitate this operation, males of most species are specially equipped with structures known as nuptial pads – rough-surfaced swellings, often heavily pigmented, which form on the outer edge of the 'thumb' of sexually active frogs and toads (plate 39). When his forelimbs encircle the female, these areas come into contact with her skin and help the male to retain his position, this being of particular importance in those species in which the male may have to fight off rival males by lashing out with his back feet while holding the female.

Nuptial pads are larger, and may extend down onto the forearm, in those species which breed in streams and torrents, and such species may also have spiny areas at the base of the arm, or patches of rough skin on

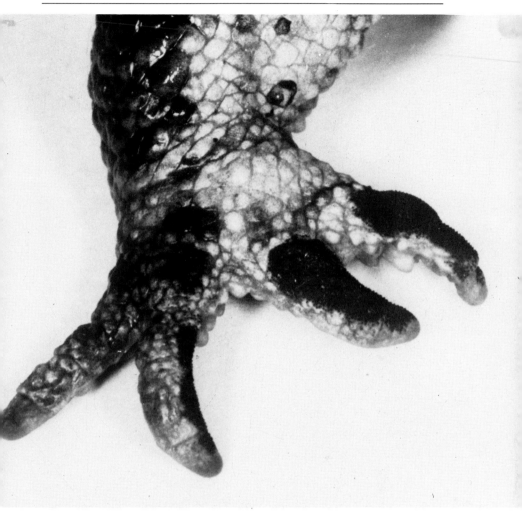

Plate 39 Nuptial pads are found in most male frogs which breed in a wet environment, although their shape and location can vary from species to species.

their chest in order to improve their grip, e.g. *Alsodes* species and some *Leptodactylus* species. Males of a number of species, e.g. *Bombina*, also have much more heavily muscled forearms for the same reason, while *Cardioglossa* species, from Africa, have greatly extended, thorny, third fingers but no nuptial pads. Terrestrial breeders often lack all of these nuptial modifications – they do not have the same difficulty in gripping the females as do aquatic breeders.

In addition to nuptial pads and spines, males of many species have glands which seem to be connected in some way with mating and egg-laying. The abdominal gland of certain obese microhylids, which secretes the 'glue' which holds the pair together, has already been mentioned. Other species have glands on the throat and inner surface of the forearm, e.g. *Kassina senegalensis* and *maculatus*; on the dorsal surface of the forearms in some ranids; on the chest, e.g. *Leptopelis* species; on the flanks of *Ptychohyla* species; and on the thighs of some ranids from Madagascar. The function of these glands is still unclear, but since they invariably

Plate 40   Sexual dimorphism is very pronounced in frogs of the genus *Osteocephalus*, especially in this species, *O. verrucigerus*, in which only the males have warty backs.

come into contact with the female during amplexus and egg-laying, they obviously play a role at this time.

Other differences between the sexes include colour (see Chapter 2) and skin texture – males of many species have rougher skin than the females, especially in *Bombina* species and in the bufonids, although in *Atelopus* species the situation is reversed – the females have small pointed warts on their flanks, whereas those of the males are rounded. The greatest difference in skin texture probably applies to the tree frogs *Osteocephalus* from Central and South America, in which the upper surfaces of the body and limbs are rough and warty in males but practically smooth in females – *O. verrucigerus* (plate 40) is an extreme example.

The cloaca of some species may be modified in one or other of the sexes. The extended cloaca of the male 'tailed' frog, *Ascaphus truei*, used in internal fertilisation, is an obvious example, while in *Mertensophryne micranotis* the cloaca of the male is surrounded by a ring of small spines, presumed to hold it in close contact with that of the female so that sperm

Plate 41   The knob-like projection on the head of *Rana plicatella* has no known function, but is found only in males.

transfer can take place. In other species the cloaca of the female is extendible, e.g. in *Pipa pipa*, in which the eggs are manoeuvred onto her back during egg-laying, while in *Kassina* species small flaps around the cloaca may help to place the eggs accurately.

Secondary sex characteristics which are not directly connected to mating and egg-laying include the tusks and spines used by males during territorial combat, as in tree frogs of the *Hyla boans* group, which have curved spines at the base of their thumbs, and in some male centrolenid and hylid frogs which have a similar spine growing from the base of their forelimbs, i.e. at the 'shoulder' (fig. 13). Tusks are present in several species of carnivorous frogs, but in *Adelotus brevis* they are much larger in males than in females and are presumably used in fighting. The row of small spines around the rim of the upper jaw of some male *Leptobrachium* species probably serves the same purpose. It is interesting to note in this respect that those males which fight for territory are invariably larger than the females, in contrast to the usual arrangement in frogs, in which the female may be almost twice as big as the male.

Sex differences of unknown significance include the larger tympanum in males of species such as *Rana catesbeiana* and *R. grylio*, and the presence of a small bone which pierces the tympanum in *Petropedates newtoni*. There also appears to be no obvious function for the bony knob-like projection growing from the skull of male *Rana plicatella* from South East Asia (plate 41).

Fig. 13 Spines, such as those on the shoulder of *Centrolenella* species (left) and hand of *Hyla rosenbergi* are found only in males and are used in territorial combat.

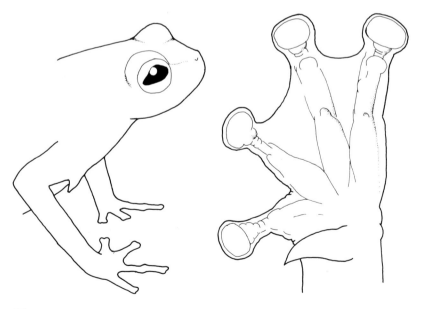

Chapter 7

Reproduction 2 – development

The egg

Amphibian 'eggs' consist of two parts: the egg itself, correctly called the ovum (plural:ova), and the surrounding jelly-like material (fig. 14). There is variation in both of these components.

The ovum consists of two sections: the animal pole, containing the cells which eventually divide and differentiate to form the embryo, and the vegetal pole, which comprises the yolk which nourishes the embryo until it begins to feed independently. In eggs that are laid in water, the animal pole is black due to a layer of pigment (melanin) which covers it, and comprises the upper hemisphere of the egg, whereas the vegetal pole is grey. It is assumed that the melanin protects the developing embryo from harmful ultra-violet rays, and may also help to raise its temperature slightly. Eggs that are laid beneath logs or in moss, etc., on the ground contain a greater proportion of yolk because the embryo relies on this source of food for a far longer time, often right up until it has

Fig. 14   A single frog egg, drawn diagrammatically.

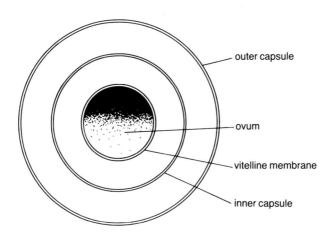

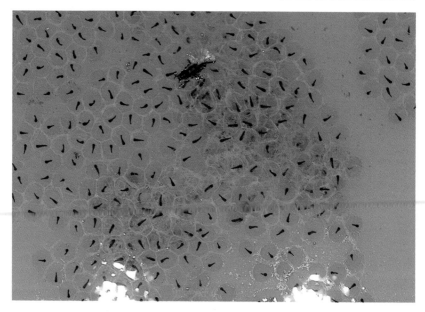

Plate 42   The eggs of many species which spawn in small bodies of water are
attached to the surface film in order to ensure that they obtain sufficient oxygen.
These belong to an undetermined Malaysian species, possibly a microhylid.

metamorphosed. In addition, the animal pole is not covered with a layer
of melanin (since the egg is not exposed to radiation) and so the whole of
the egg is much paler in colour, usually creamy.

Eggs that are usually laid on vegetation overhanging streams may
also be pale if they are attached to the underside of a leaf or if a leaf is
wrapped around them (as in plate 54), but if they are in an exposed
position the melanin layer will be present and they will be dark in
colour. The eggs of a few species, such as some *Centrolenella* species and
the New Guinean tree frog *Litoria iris*, which spawn on leaves, have
green yolks and are therefore well camouflaged.

Unlike the eggs of higher animals, i.e. reptiles and birds, amphibian
ova are not enclosed in a shell, but derive a certain amount of protection
from layers of jelly-like matter which surround them. In frogs, the jelly
layers are contained in from one to four concentric membranes known as
vitelline membranes, the exact configuration depending on species. The
jelly protects the ovum from attack by mould and other harmful micro-
organisms and from physical damage caused by water movement, and so

Plate 43   Several ranids from cooler climates produce large rafts of spawn in the
shallow parts of ponds – this is believed to conserve heat and so speed up the
development of the eggs.

on. In some species, e.g. *Bufo*, it may also contain distasteful substances which discourage fish, etc., from eating the eggs. The jelly, which is virtually colourless, is secreted by the female as the eggs are laid and swells considerably once it comes into contact with water. Thus in aquatic-type eggs the total diameter of the outer membrane in some species may be four times the diameter of the ovum itself, although other species lay eggs which contain only a thin layer of jelly. The size of the ovum is related to the species concerned and its reproductive mode – terrestrial eggs are large and have less jelly surrounding them, although the outermost membrane is much tougher than in aquatic eggs. Within a given mode of reproduction, small frogs lay small eggs and, for a given size of frog, the later its egg hatches, the larger the egg (see also the section on parental care).

The clutch

The arrangement of the clutch varies with the species. In the simplest form of egg-laying, e.g. *Xenopus* species, the eggs are scattered singly over the substrate and may become attached to stones, twigs or aquatic plants, or they may float just below the surface, e.g. in *Hymenochirus*. In other species the eggs are laid in a single large clump, e.g. *Rana temporaria* (plate 2), or in several small clumps attached to aquatic plants, e.g. *Hyperolius marmoratus* (plate 44) and many small hylids. The benefit of laying large clumps is that the egg-masses conserve heat, and this type of spawn is therefore most common amongst frogs that live in cool places. The heat-retaining properties may be further enhanced by the aggrega-

Plate 44   Eggs of *Hyperolius marmoratus* which, like many similar species, are laid in several small clumps, attached to aquatic vegetation.

Plate 45   The eggs of bufonids are typically laid in necklace-like strings, often entangled amongst aquatic plants.

tion of several clumps in one part of the pond, so forming large 'rafts' (as in Plate 43). Toads of the genus *Bufo*, and some related species, lay their eggs in long strings – each string contains a double row of ova, one from each oviduct (plate 45) although once the jelly has swollen their position may alter so that they appear as a single row. As the eggs are laid, the toads move about and so entangle the strings amongst aquatic vegetation, etc.

Species which breed in small, temporary bodies of water often attach their eggs to the surface film (plate 42). Only in this way will the developing larvae obtain sufficient oxygen from the otherwise oxygen-depleted water.

Eggs which are laid on land or which are carried by a parent may be laid singly, in which case they are usually sticky and so form clumps or clusters, or they may be linked together in short strings, sometimes joined by a constriction in the jelly or, in some microhylids from New Guinea at least, by a short length of thread-like mucus.

Clutch sizes range from one in the tiny *Sminthillus limbatus* and three to six in several other small terrestrial breeding species, and up to 30,000 or more in large toads such as *Bufo marinus*. Medium sized species commonly have clutch sizes which are within the range 500–5,000, but there is great variation.

Foam nests

A very specialised kind of clutch involves depositing the eggs in a mass of froth or foam, and this method has arisen independently in several families in widely separated parts of the world. Foam nests are formed by the whipping up of water, the mucus surrounding the eggs, and air, and this is sometimes performed by the male, sometimes by the female, and sometimes by both. Various theories have been proposed as to the function of the foam, including protection of the eggs from predators, preventing the eggs from drying up, absorbing heat, reflecting heat (!), and buffering the pH of the eggs' micro-environment. Foam nests may be constructed on the water, on land or in trees and bushes – in this respect they parallel three basic modes of reproduction in other frogs and toads and will be dealt with in more detail in the following chapter.

Plate 46   The foam nest of *Physalaemus pustulosus*, measuring about 40 mm in diameter and sitting in a few millimetres of water.

Development

Development of the egg begins with the division of the ovum into two halves, which in turn divide successively to give rise to 4, 8, 16, 32-cell stages and so on. The animal cells gradually grow right around the area of yolk and slowly absorb this as the embryo forms. The larva emerges from the protective layer of jelly at various stages depending on the species – in the 'conventional', aquatic-breeding frogs and toads, it wriggles free before the limbs have made an appearance and at about the same time as the mouth begins to form (plate 48). Larvae of terrestrial breeders or of species which lay their eggs on vegetation usually remain within the egg until a later stage (delayed hatching) or even until metamorphosis has taken place (direct development). In order to free themselves from the protective membrane(s), the larvae produce enzymes which break down the material and, in *Eleutherodactylus*, a small egg-tooth also forms to enable the froglet to cut its way out of the tough outer membrane.

The rate at which the eggs develop is dependent on temperature. As is to be expected, the eggs of species from cool regions require less warmth

Plate 47   The first visible stage of development in frog eggs: the ovum has elongated to become kidney, or comma, shaped.

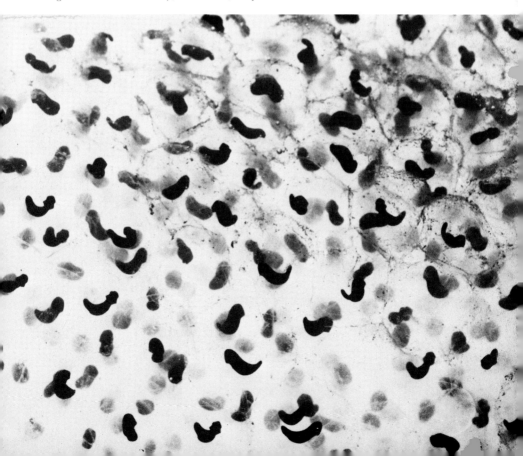

Plate 48   On hatching, the tadpoles' gills are visible, but will soon become covered by a flap of skin which grows back from the cheek region.

Plate 49   This bullfrog tadpole has well-developed, but small, hind legs.

Plate 50   Development of the front legs takes place beneath the operculum. In this *Ololygon rubra* tadpole the right 'elbow' is beginning to emerge through the spiracle.

97

Plate 51   Many young frogs leave the water before their tails are completely absorbed, as in this young *Hyla geographica.*

than those from warm ones, although eggs of all species will tolerate quite a wide range of temperatures. However, the eggs of few species, even those from cool regions, will develop if the temperature drops below about 5°C and few warm-adapted species can tolerate temperatures greater than about 32°C – the ideal temperature for tropical and sub-tropical species seems to be about 25°C, for temperate species about 15°C. Generally speaking, the eggs of temperate species develop at a much slower rate than those of tropical ones.

There are also limits to the amount of salinity and acidity which the eggs can tolerate, and the values of these factors will also depend on the environment to which the various species have adapted. Thus, the eggs of species which live near the coast, e.g. some populations of *Bufo calamita*, are likely to tolerate a greater degree of salinity than those of species which live far inland.

Although embryologists recognise up to 46 stages in the transition from single-celled egg to metamorphosis, many of these are only distinguishable by microscopic examination. The most obvious events are:

a)   Single cell begins to divide (about 30–60 minutes after laying).
b)   Embryo begins to elongate.
c)   Embryo becomes comma-shaped (plate 47).
d)   External gills appear, mouth forms. Tadpole hatches (if aquatic) and clings to jelly-mass, aquatic plants or surface (plate 48).
e)   Flap of skin (operculum) grows over gills. Tadpole is free-swimming and feeding by now.
f)   Hindlimbs appear (plate 49).
g)   Forelimbs appear, left one emerging through spiracle in the commonest type of tadpole (plate 50).
h)   Mouth changes shape as tadpole becomes more frog-like in appearance.
i)   Tail becomes smaller, tadpole may leave water at this stage (plate 51).
j)   Tail completely absorbed, metamorphosis complete.

The tadpole

Free-living larvae, having absorbed their yolk supplies, must begin to feed and a variety of feeding methods and apparatus are used to achieve this (see Chapter 5). These are known as adaptive variations because they are dependent on the environment and habits of the tadpole. Morphological variations consist of four basic types of tadpoles. Although there is some correlation between each tadpole type and its evolutionary position, the link is not yet fully understood. The types are classified according to the arrangement of their respiratory and feeding

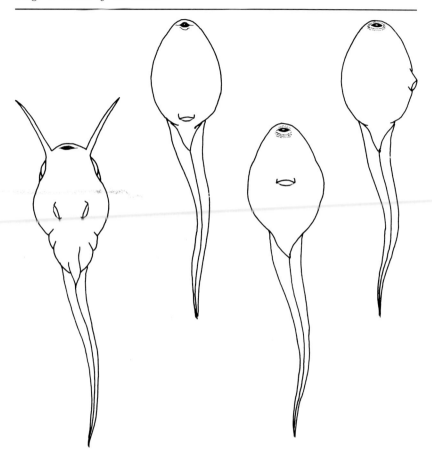

Fig. 15   Tadpole Types I–IV. Type I tadpoles occur in the Pipidae and Rhinophrynidae, Type II in the Microhylidae, Type III in the Leiopelmatidae and Discoglossidae. All other families have Type IV tadpoles.

mechanism and can be distinguished externally by the position of the spiracle. Figure 15 illustrates each type and lists the families to which each corresponds.

Although the growth rate of the tadpole depends to a large extent on the temperature of the water, there is great variation, even amongst tadpoles from the same clutch. In addition, species which live in arid regions, where pools of water are temporary, develop very quickly in order to metamorphose before they are left high and dry. For example, spadefoot toad tadpoles, *Scaphiopus* species, may complete their development and leave the water within two weeks and a similarly rapid rate of development has been recorded for species which live in the same type of environment in Africa and Australia. At the other extreme, species which develop in cold mountain streams can take up to three years to complete their development, e.g. *Ascaphus truei* in North America and *Heleophryne* species in southern Africa. Species from cold regions in North America and Europe frequently spend one winter at least as tadpoles and metamorphose in their second year. The majority of frogs, however, metamorphose in two to three months.

The behaviour of tadpoles has not been well studied although even casual observations show that there are differences between species. Some show a type of shoaling behaviour, e.g. *Hyla geographica* and *Pyxicephalus adspersus*, by means of which they may increase their food supply by stirring up detritus from the bottom, or reduce predation, and in one species at least, *Leptodactylus ocellatus*, shoaling is associated with parental guarding. Other tadpoles, e.g. those of *Alytes obstetricans* and *Gastrotheca riobambae*, spend much time hanging tail-down from the surface of ponds, but dive down when disturbed. The response to possible predators varies tremendously: some species appear to ignore disturbance completely, whereas others are very alert and dart away rapidly, sometimes hiding beneath rocks, etc. Again, some are protectively coloured and difficult to see against a background of mud or stones while others are very conspicuous.

The ultimate size of the tadpoles obviously depends on the size of the adults, but may also depend on the food supply. The hormones which control development are not completely dependent on growth rate, however, and may induce metamorphosis at a small size even if optimum growth has not been achieved. On the other hand, metamorphosis may be delayed until the tadpole has reached an abnormally large size, usually due to an absence of iodine which is necessary to produce the required hormone, thyroxin. Certain species grow into enormous tadpoles before metamorphosing into moderate sized adults – *Pseudis paradoxus* is noteworthy in this respect as its tadpole may grow to 200 mm and then 'shrink' to 70 mm at metamorphosis. It was this size discrepancy which confused early scientists into thinking that it reversed the normal course of events in frog development: they believed that the large tadpole developed from the small frog and named it the 'paradoxical' frog accordingly.

Metamorphosis

At metamorphosis the young frog is ready to leave the water (assuming that it is not an aquatic species). It may do this straight away or wait until nightfall or for rainy weather. Tadpoles of a midwife toad, *Alytes cisternasi*, apparently leave the water and burrow into the soil before their tail is completely absorbed and other species, such as the spadefoot toads, must also get beneath the surface quickly or they will dry up in their arid environment. Young tree frogs usually climb into reeds and pond-side vegetation as they emerge, frequently doing so before their tails are completely gone (plate 51), while other species disperse over a wide area and their movements between this time and their first breeding season, one to four years later, are largely unknown. European common frogs and common toads, *Rana temporaria* and *Bufo bufo*, may be forced to remain in or around their pond for an extended period of dry weather and then all leave *en masse* during a rain storm – predation is especially heavy at this time with a wide variety of small mammals and birds benefiting from an abundant and defenceless food supply, while in some species, notably the African bullfrog, *Pyxicephalus adspersus*, the emerging young prey heavily on one another.

Chapter 8
Life-histories

The life-cycle of a frog or toad comprises a sequence of events starting with the urge to breed and finishing with the metamorphosis and growth of individuals forming the next generation. As we have already seen, almost every stage in this sequence is subject to variation, with the result that there are many possible permutations of the events which make up a complete life-cycle. The purpose of this section is to describe all of the known reproductive modes of frogs, from the moment of egg-laying through to metamorphosis.

In Europe and North America, where there are relatively few species of frogs, the majority spawn in open bodies of water – ponds, lakes and ditches – where the tadpole can continue its development in the normal way. Where more than one species lives in an area it is usually the case that each has slightly different preferences for the exact location of its spawn; thus in Britain there are three species of frogs: the common frog, *Rana temporaria*, usually spawns in small pools, including garden ponds, or in the shallow bays of larger ones; the common toad, *Bufo bufo*, may use the same ponds but lays its eggs in the deeper parts; while the natterjack toad, *Bufo calamita*, is confined to shallow, often temporary bodies of water, such as those which form behind sand dunes. In this way they avoid some of the competition which would otherwise exist between their tadpoles, demonstrating one aspect of a principle known as 'habitat partitioning'.

In other parts of the world, especially the tropics, many more than three species often occur together – the highest number recorded so far was in a part of Amazonian Ecuador, where eighty-one species were found to inhabit a few acres of forest. Obviously, if these species are to avoid undue competition, some of them need to be very ingenious indeed. One way round the problem is for some to spawn at different times of the year from the others, i.e. there may be wet season and dry season breeders (temporal partitioning), but this still leaves many species breeding together. Superimposed on this pattern of habitat or temporal partitioning is the one of varying requirements of each species, such as temperature and food supply, the desire to minimise predation, or the total absence of conventional breeding sites in some places. It is this complex interplay of so many factors which has resulted in the enormous diversity of reproductive modes in frogs.

Several systems have been used by previous authors to classify reproductive modes: the one used here takes the trend towards terrestriality as its main theme, starting with methods which depend heavily on water at all stages of development, and moving in steps towards methods in which water is completely unnecessary. It will be seen that in some groups of closely related animals the trend is very obvious, whereas others are more conservative – this probably reflects the amount of environmental pressures which are applied to these respective groups. Looking at the situation from another angle, it is interesting to note that, in several cases, similar modes have evolved independently in species which are widely separated both taxonomically and geographically, so that there are some genera in which two or three different modes are used, whereas similar reproductive modes may be used by species which are not closely related. Where it is not possible to list all of the species which use a particular method, the examples given reflect the geographic and taxonomic width of that particular category.

Due to its complexity, the information which is given in the following section is summarised in the chart on page 126.

Eggs laid in water: aquatic tadpoles

It is assumed that this common method of breeding is primitive in frogs and that departures from it represent adaptations to unfavourable conditions. The main variations within this method involve the use of different types of aquatic site.

1) Large permanent bodies of water

This is the system which will be familiar to most of the readers of this book. Roughly half of the known species of frogs breed in this way. Even here, however, there may be variation in the way in which the eggs are deposited: they may be laid in clumps, strings or singly; they may be attached to aquatic vegetation, to the substrate of the pond, or they may float; and they may all be laid together or in several small batches.

A detailed account of the various types of spawn is given on page 92, and the subsequent development of the tadpoles is described on page 95. All four morphological types of tadpole may be found amongst the species in this category.

2) Small temporary pools

A number of species use small puddles, hoof-prints, wheel ruts, etc., for egg-laying. These sites have the advantage that they are unlikely to contain aquatic predators or competing tadpoles, and they are often in plentiful supply. In the tropical rain belt these pools rarely dry out completely due to frequent rain, and so the main problem is one of low oxygen. Species such as *Microhyla*, *Hyla*, *Ololygon*, etc., attach their eggs to the surface film in order to overcome this and their tadpoles often have enlarged gills and may spend much of their time near the surface, where oxygen exchange is maximal. In temperate regions a few montane species such as *Bombina variegata* use similar sites: here the rainfall is also sufficient to keep the pools topped up, and the cooler water contains plenty of oxygen. In desert regions, however, temporary pools rarely last very long and species such as *Scaphiopus* and *Rhinophrynus* in North America and *Pelobates* in southern Europe, have tadpoles which develop rapidly in order to metamorphose before their pools evaporate.

3) Streams and torrents

We can assume that of the frogs which are adapted to living in streams and torrents, at least some will attach their eggs to stones, etc., although this is difficult to establish and is only confirmed for a few species, including *Ascaphus truei*, the tailed frog. Other species are known to move into backwaters and spray pools in order to spawn. Torrent-adapted tadpoles are streamlined in shape and many possess suckers with which they cling to rocks (fig. 4 and plate 63), but other tadpoles live in the spaces between the gravel which forms the substrate in wide shallow streams.

4) Arboreal pools

A number of arboreal frogs make use of the small pools of water which collect between the leaves of plants, in tree-holes or in bamboo stems. In South and Central America, epiphytic plants of the family Bromeliaceae collect water in their central vases and these provide homes for a number of specialised aquatic animals, including frog larvae. By virtue of their arboreal habits, frogs of the family Hylidae, including *Hyla zeteki, H. bromeliacea, Amphodus auratus* and *Anotheca spinosa*, are the main exploiters

Fig. 16 Specialised tadpole of *Mertensophryne* and *Stephopaedes*.

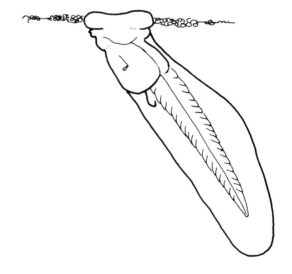

of this niche, but a bufonid, *Dendrophryniscus brevipollicatus*, and a centrolenid, *Centrolenella buckleyi*, are also known to use this type of site.

In the Old World there are no bromeliads, but plants such as tree-
ferns and certain palms collect water in their leaf-axils, while bamboo
and hollow tree-trunks also provide suitable sites. Species which lay their
eggs in these places include several Asian frogs belonging to the family
Rhacophoridae such as *Theloderma stellatum*, *Rhacophorus harrissoni*, and an
unidentified *Philautus* species. Several of these species are suspected of
feeding more or less exclusively on frog eggs, either laid for that purpose
by the female, or opportunistically on the eggs of other species which
come along afterwards. Other tree-hole breeders get around the problem
of food by supplying their tadpoles with sufficient yolk to nourish them
until they metamorphose. This group of frogs is described under a later
heading.

In Africa, two small bufonids, *Mertensophryne micranotis* and *Stephopaedes
anotis*, lay their eggs in the pools of water which collect between the
buttress roots of large trees or in crevices in dead trees, and their highly
unusual tadpoles (fig. 16) probably feed on the algal or bacterial film
which grows on the bark.

5) Specially constructed basins

In South America a group of large tree frogs, *Hyla boans*, *H. faber* and *H.
rosenbergi*, spawn in shallow depressions made by the male. These are
scooped out in the mud, sand or gravel at the edge of a stream or pond
and fill with water through seepage. The males call from their 'nests'
and encourage females to approach and lay eggs, and each male defends
his territory vigorously if another male attempts to take it over. The eggs
are attached to the surface of the water and the tadpoles, when they
hatch, hang down with their enlarged gills in contact with the water.
Some basins contain eggs and/or larvae in various stages of development, which indicates that the male may attract a series of females over
several nights. The larvae are eventually released by a rise in water level
and in this way they gain access to a more extensive area over which to
feed.

In Malaysia a ranid, *Rana plicatella*, lays its eggs in small (2.5–3 mm
diameter) crater-like 'nests' of mud (plate 53). The eggs hatch after a
few days, by which time the structure has begun to disintegrate due to
constant seepage of water around it. The tadpoles appear to develop
normally and presumably wriggle into nearby streams or pools once they
become active. Another ranid, *Rana blythi*, from Borneo, spawns in
shallow depressions made by the male in gravel bars in forest streams.

6) Foam nests floating on water

Some frogs belonging to the Leptodactylidae, e.g. *Leptodactylus ocellatus*,
and also the Myobatrachidae, e.g. several *Limnodynastes* species, construct
foam nests on the surface of open water. Other species such as those of

Plate 52 Males of *Hyla rosenbergi* and a few closely related species build basin-shaped nests in which to spawn once they have attracted a mate. Each nest is vigorously defended against intruding males.

Plate 53 *Rana plicatella* lays small clutches of eggs in crater-shaped nests of mud.

the genus *Physalaemus*, construct their nests over small bodies of water, often temporary, rain-filled depressions. A basic difference exists between the two families in the way in which the nest is formed. In leptodactylids (American) the foam is created by kicking movements of the hind limbs of the male and/or female, whereas in the myobatrachids (Australasian) the foam is produced from bubbles made by the female's *front* limbs – the digits on these become slightly frilled at breeding time and while she lays her eggs she paddles rapidly with them, forcing air down into the water and passing it under her body. The bubbles accumulate around the eggs and the male does not contribute to the nest-building. In both methods, the mucus surrounding the eggs adds strength to the bubbles, enabling the nest to last for several days, often long after the eggs have hatched. The tadpoles swim away from the nest and develop in the normal way.

Eggs laid out of water: aquatic tadpoles

The first step towards terrestriality is the laying of eggs out of the water, but which hatch into normal aquatic tadpoles which fall or make their way to water to continue development in the normal way. Again, a number of distinct sites are used by species in this category.

1) Tadpoles drop into water on hatching

The technique of attaching eggs to leaves, etc., which hang over water into which the tadpoles drop may seem chancy, but it has evolved in many species from at least five families.

The majority of the tree frogs belonging to the sub-family Phyllomedusinae, comprising about forty species in the genera *Agalychnis*, *Pachymedusa* and *Phyllomedusa*, all from Central and South America, mate in bushes and low trees at the edge of pools and lay a gelatinous mass of eggs on a large leaf which may then be folded around them. The male may be responsible for folding the leaf in some species but, in *Phyllomedusa trinitatus* at least, it seems that the female does most of the work, moving slowly up the leaf as the eggs are laid, gripping its outer edges with her hind feet and pulling them over to form a tube around the eggs (plate 55). At the top and bottom of the tube, 'empty' jelly-masses are laid to plug the openings of the tube. This presumably prevents the eggs from drying out and may also offer some protection from ants, parasitic flies and other predators. The tadpoles hatch about six days later and wriggle down through the jelly to drop into the water. A number of other South American hylids, including *Hyla favosa*, *H. leucophyllata* and related species, also lay their eggs on overhanging vegetation and at least one species from New Guinea, *Litoria iris*, lays small clumps of bright green eggs on leaves overhanging streams.

With two known exceptions, *Centrolenella buckleyi* and *Centrolene geckoideum*, the 'glass frogs' of the family Centrolenidae all attach their eggs to the upper or lower sides of large leaves overhanging streams. The male often stays with the eggs until they hatch and he may attract other females to the same site and so fertilise a second clutch positioned close to the first. *Centrolene geckoideum* differs by laying its eggs on rocks or roots rather than vegetation, but these too hatch into tadpoles which drop or slide down into streams.

In Africa, the little leaf-folding frogs, genus *Afrixalus*, all apparently lay their eggs on emergent vegetation – reeds, grasses, etc. – as do some species of *Hyperolius* from the same family (Hyperoliidae). As the eggs

Plate 54   The leaf-folding frogs, *Phyllomedusa* and *Agalychnis*, as well as other species, attach their eggs to leaves hanging over pools. These *P. trinitatus* are nearing the end of egg-laying and as they slowly move up the leaf the female pulls its edges around the eggs to form a tube-like structure.

Plate 55   (Opposite) The completed nest of *Phyllomedusa trinitatus*. Note that the eggs contain no black pigment because they will not be exposed to damaging ultra-violet radiation.

hatch the tadpoles begin to move about and this causes the mucus containing them to slide gradually down into the water – but in *Hyperolius obstetricans* the female stays with the eggs and kicks the tadpoles into the water when they hatch. The Madagascan ranids belonging to the genus *Mantidactylus* also breed in this way – *M. liber* lays 30–90 eggs on a leaf, usually about 1–1.5 metres above water. The tadpoles hatch and drop into the water 5–7 days later.

Members of the Rhacophoridae from Asia and Africa also lay their eggs above ground level, but in foam nests. *Chiromantis xerampelina* from Africa creates a large circular nest of foam several metres above the surface of ponds and lakes. The outer surface dries in the sun to produce a crust which protects the eggs from desiccation and the movement of the hatching tadpoles causes this to break down when they are ready to leave the nest. *C. petersi* may form gigantic foam nests as a result of several pairs spawning communally on the same branch, and instances of extra males accompanying a spawning pair and adding their foam and, presumably, sperm, to its nest have been recorded for this species.

The Asian *Polypedates leucomystax* makes its foam nest amongst emergent vegetation, on tree-stumps or artificial sites above water (plate 56). Nest construction takes most of the night and the adults are often found putting the finishing touches to their nest early the next morning. The remains of several dozen nests may be found at certain favoured sites. Hatching and subsequent development of the tadpoles takes place a few days later although in places the nests are heavily parasitised by fly larvae. A related species *Rhacophorus. dennysi*, is reported to form communal foam nests in the same way as *Chiromantis petersi*.

A single species of hyperoliid, *Opisthothylax immaculatus*, from Africa, builds a small foam nest amongst reeds, etc., and this is then covered by folded leaves.

2) Eggs laid on land which subsequently becomes flooded

In the simplest form of terrestrial breeding, eggs are laid on land which is prone to flooding. The Australian myobatrachids *Pseudophryne bibroni*, *P. dendyi* and *P. semimarmorata* breed communally in damp grassland. The males call from small depressions and females lay small batches of eggs in these over a period of several nights. The male stays with the eggs for a while and they begin to develop, but do not hatch until rain floods the area. Development may be arrested and hatching delayed for as long as 30–40 days if sufficient rain does not fall. Other frogs which lay their eggs in similar situations are some of the *Geocrinia* species, which are also myobatrachids from Australia, and *Rana adenopleura* from Asia.

3) Eggs laid on land: tadpoles wriggle to water

A slightly more sophisticated method is used by species which lay their eggs near water and, on hatching, the larvae wriggle across the surface until they enter it and continue their development there. Examples of this mode are found amongst the Ranidae, e.g. *Rana magna*; the Lepto-dactylidae, e.g. *Batrachyla* species; the Myobatrachidae, e.g. *Mixophyes* species; and the Hyperoliidae, e.g. *Leptopelis* species. In the latter, males call from burrows at the water's edge and the female lays her eggs there. When they hatch, the tadpoles first wriggle to the surface before making their way to water.

4) Eggs laid in burrow, female digs tunnel to water

The African ranids belonging to the genus *Hemisus* are rotund burrowing frogs which mate and spawn beneath the ground. In one species (*H. marmoratus*) at least, the female stays with her eggs until they begin to hatch and digs a sloping tunnel connecting the nest chamber with the bank of a nearby pool. The tadpoles, through their wriggling move-ments, gradually slide down the tunnel and into the water.

5) Eggs laid on land, tadpoles carried to water

As far as is known, all of the poison dart frogs, *Dendrobates* and *Phyllo-bates*, as well as the related *Colostethus* species, lay their eggs on land, usually on a leaf or a small area of ground which they have carefully cleaned. They are then visited or guarded by one or both parents until they hatch. At this point the attending parent encourages them to wriggle up onto its back and carries them to a suitable place for the continuation of their development. The number of larvae carried in this way ranges from 1 to 35 or more, and although it is usually the males which do the carrying, in some species, e.g. *Dendrobates pumilio*, it is always the females. The larvae may remain on the adult's back for a few minutes or for several hours, and are firmly attached by a mucus secretion which is only broken down by immersion in water – in this way there is no danger of the tadpoles becoming detached accidentally. Small forest streams are the usual destination of the larvae, but several species, e.g. *D. pumilio* and *D. histrionicus*, take their young to small pools of water amongst bromeliad leaves or in the leaf-axils of other forest plants. In Hawaii, *D. auratus*, which has been introduced, uses the water which collects in broken bottles and other artificial breeding sites for accommo-dating its tadpoles.

Apart from the dendrobatids, tadpole-carrying with the subsequent release of the tadpoles into water is known in a ranid, *Rana finchi*, from Borneo, and in *Rhinoderma rufum*, which carries the tadpoles in its mouth (see page 119).

6) Eggs carried by parents, tadpoles aquatic

A variation of the previous system is to carry the eggs from the time they are laid rather than depositing them on the ground. Several methods seemed to have been 'tried out'.

Males of three species of discoglossids from Europe, *Alytes obstetricans*,

Plate 56   A pair of Asian tree frogs, *Polypedates leucomystax*, putting the finishing touches to their foam nest, attached, in this case, to the walls of a disused concrete water tank.

Plate 57   (Opposite) A female marsupial frog, *Gastrotheca riobambae*, having carried her eggs for three to four months, releases her tadpoles into shallow water. From time to time she uses her back feet to scoop them out of the pouch.

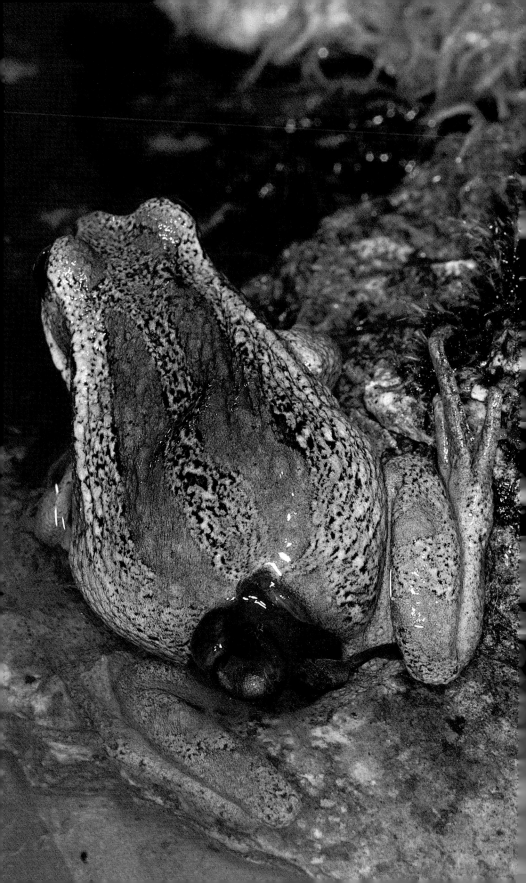

Plate 58   Male *Alytes obstetricans*, the midwife toad, carry strings of eggs until the tadpoles are ready to hatch.

A. cisternasii and *A. muletensis*, carry their eggs wrapped around their back legs. *Alytes* mates on the land and, as the eggs are laid, the male moves forward on the female's back and moves his hind legs until the string of eggs is entwined around them (plate 58). He carries them in this way for about one month, visiting a pool or puddle as necessary in order to prevent them from drying out, and when they are due to hatch he goes to a pool and releases the tadpoles. Exact details of *A. muletensis'* life-history are still unknown. Their activities have earned these toads the popular name of 'midwife toads'.

Females carry their eggs on their backs in two unrelated families of frogs: the Pipidae and the Hylidae. Variations on this method concern the environments where the frogs live (the Pipidae are aquatic, whereas the egg-carrying hylids are terrestrial/arboreal) and the stage at which the offspring are released, which may be as larvae or fully metamor-phosed young (in which case they are dealt with under a different heading, page 123).

Among the pipids, egg-carrying is restricted to the seven South American species belonging to the genus *Pipa*. Egg-laying involves a complicated sequence of movements in which the paired animals swim towards the surface of the water and turn over at the top of the loop. A few eggs are laid during each turnover and these are manoeuvred onto the back of the female as the pair completes its loop and comes to rest on the substrate, the male using his large hind feet to gently push them towards the centre of the female's back. This manoeuvre is repeated until the full complement of eggs is laid. During the next twenty-four hours a pad of sponge-like tissue swells around the eggs until each is almost totally embedded. Each egg then develops within its cell until the time of release. In *Pipa carvalhoi* this occurs two to four weeks later, by which time the eggs have developed into small filter-feeding tadpoles.

Amongst the Hylidae, *Gastrotheca riobambae* and some other *Gastrotheca* species spawn on land and, as the eggs are laid, the male directs them with his back feet into a pouch situated on the female's back. One hundred or more eggs may be laid and stored in this way, making the back of the female appear swollen (plate 57). The eggs are carried for three to four months, by which time they have hatched and grown into large tadpoles. The female takes her brood to a suitable pool or ditch and uses the toes of her back feet to hold the pouch open and scoop out the tadpoles, which then develop in the normal way.

Eggs laid in or out of water: tadpoles develop without feeding

The first step towards terrestrial breeding was the laying of eggs on land, but in the methods described so far it is still necessary for the tadpoles to continue their development in water in order to feed. This category, therefore, represents an important intermediate stage between terrestrial and aquatic breeding – the tadpoles, though not fully terrestrial in many cases, are provided with enough yolk to enable them to develop until metamorphosis without needing to feed.

1) Tadpoles remain in nest

Several species lay terrestrial eggs, the tadpoles of which develop *in situ*. Others lay their eggs in very small bodies of water which may not contain very much food (but which do not contain predators either). Too much emphasis should not be placed on the difference between aquatic and terrestrial breeding sites within this group. The opportunity to produce terrestrial tadpoles is limited to species living in areas of constant high humidity – those species living in areas which are subject to dry spells are obliged to lay their eggs in a small quantity of water in order to prevent them from desiccating.

The microhylids belonging to the genus *Breviceps*, from Africa, lay their eggs in underground chambers and, in some species at least, they hatch non-feeding tadpoles. Several ranids from Africa, including *Arthroleptis hewitti* and *A. lightfooti*, lay their eggs in burrows or depressions in the ground. Of the three species of leiopelmatid frogs from New Zealand,

Plate 59 *Kalophrynus pleurostigma*, a South East Asian microhylid which lays its eggs in a small depression, where they hatch into non-feeding tadpoles.

one, *Leiopelma hochstetteri*, lays clusters of 2–11 eggs in damp places beneath stones or decaying vegetation. After three to four weeks an advanced tadpole hatches from each and this continues to develop, drawing on its yolk reserves, until it is fully metamorphosed. Other non-feeding tadpoles complete their development in terrestrial foam nests, e.g. the two species of *Kyarranus* and *Philoria frosti* from Australia and the six species of *Adenomera* and *Leptodactylus fallax* from South America.

Some of the microhylids from Madagascar belonging to the genera *Platyhyla*, *Plethodontohyla* and *Anodontohyla*, lay small clutches of eggs in tree-holes, hollow bamboo stems and leaf-axils and, although the tad-poles are aquatic, they do not feed. Another microhylid, *Kalophrynus pleurostigma* from Borneo and peninsular Malaysia, breeds in water-filled cavities in rotting logs or in small depressions on the forest floor, where its tadpoles develop without feeding, and in Africa a small bufonid, *Nectophrynoides malcomi*, has a similar system.

2) Tadpoles carried by parent

In three totally unrelated species, eggs are laid on land and then picked up by a parent as they hatch. The methods are completely different and must therefore be treated separately.

In Australia, a small frog belonging to the family Myobatrachidae carries its tadpoles in slit-like pouches in its groin region: *Assa darlingtoni* comes from Queensland and New South Wales, where it inhabits damp places beneath stones, etc. The female lays about ten eggs on damp leaves or amongst moss and the male visits these when they begin to hatch. By shuffling his body amongst them he stimulates the tadpoles to wriggle over his body until they find the opening to one or other of the pouches. Once they are installed there they complete their development and emerge as fully formed froglets.

Darwin's frog, *Rhinoderma darwini*, which comes from the beech forests of southern Chile and Argentina, lays small clusters of terrestrial eggs, usually numbering 30–40. The male stays near the eggs and when the tadpoles begin to move about inside the jelly he picks them up in his mouth and they remain in his vocal pouch for about three weeks, when they are fully developed. He then spits them out. Recent research indi-cates that the developing tadpoles may obtain some nourishment from secretions which the male produces inside the pouch. The only other species in the family, *Rhinoderma rufum*, has a similar system, but ejects his tadpoles into water, where they continue to develop in the normal way.

Sooglossus seychellensis differs from the two species described above in that the female, not the male, carries the tadpoles. The eggs are apparently laid on land and the tadpoles climb onto the back of the parent when they hatch, in much the same way as those of the dendro-batid frogs. However, in *Sooglossus*, the tadpoles remain on the parent's back until they have metamorphosed.

3) Eggs carried, non-feeding tadpoles released into water

The marsupial frogs belonging to the genera *Flectonotus* and *Fritziana* carry their eggs and tadpoles until they have developed their hind limbs, then release them into a small body of water, usually a bromeliad vase, where they continue to grow and metamorphose without needing to feed. The two species of *Fritziana* carry their eggs in a small hollow on their back, but in *Flectonotus* they are enclosed in a slit-like pouch which seems to be a transitional stage towards the development of the fully enclosed pouch of the *Gastrotheca* species. Egg-laying has been observed in *Flectonotus pygmaeus*, which comes from Venezuela. While in amplexus, the male rests with both of his back feet inside the female's pouch. As each egg is laid he catches it between his heels, fertilises it and then pushes it into the pouch. This performance is repeated for each egg, the entire clutch numbering about ten.

4) Eggs and tadpoles carried by parent

Considering the number of species which carry their eggs and the number which carry their larvae, it is quite surprising that, as far as is known, members of only one genus carry both eggs *and* larvae.

One of the most unexpected methods of reproduction in frogs only came to light in 1974. A female *Rheobatrachus silus*, a small aquatic frog from Queensland, Australia, which had only been known to science since the previous year, disgorged several young from its mouth after behaving abnormally in its aquarium. Subsequent dissection of this animal showed that its stomach was abnormally large and distended. It appears that females 'eat' their own eggs at some point after they are laid (exactly when is not known), and these then develop for the next six to seven weeks in her stomach, which changes in form to a sac-like organ which takes up most of the body cavity. The tadpoles have sufficient yolk to complete their development but during this gestation period the female is unable to feed, the mechanism for secreting digestive juices having been 'switched off' by a chemical produced by the tadpoles in order to prevent it from acting on them. When the young are fully formed, they are forcibly ejected from the female's mouth – amazing!

Tragically, within six years, *R. silus* had disappeared from its habitat and could well be extinct, but by a strange coincidence a second species, *R. vitellinus*, was discovered in 1984, just two months after the last *R. silus* died in captivity. This frog too broods its young in its stomach, although details appear to differ slightly, and, as with *R. silus*, the new species lives in a very restricted area.

The breeding habits of these two closely related frogs, one possibly extinct, is unique, not only amongst frogs, but amongst all vertebrates.

Eggs laid out of water: direct development without tadpoles

Many species of frogs and toads from a remarkably wide range of geographical locations and families have evolved a method of reproduction which skips the tadpole stage altogether. The eggs of these species have tough outer membranes and contain all of the nutrients which the embryo will require, and so it is able to complete its development, right up until metamorphosis, within the egg capsule. Direct development has many advantages: it does away with a stage which is very vulnerable to predation; it enables frogs to live and breed in areas where there is little or no standing water, especially in rain forests and cloud forests; and it makes guarding the brood relatively easy.

1) Eggs laid on land

A multitude of varied frogs breed in this way but two groups stand out as the specialists: almost all 400 or so species of *Eleutherodactylus* from Central and South America and the West Indies; and all eighty-six species of microhylids found on the island of New Guinea (comprising 47 per cent of all known frogs there). *Eleutherodactylus* and several other closely related genera of leptodactylids lay small clusters of relatively large eggs amongst leaf-litter, moss or on the leaves of plants. These may be guarded by a parent or left. *E. johnstonei*, from the West Indies, lays about 25 eggs at a time, and these take about 12 to 14 days to hatch.

The New Guinean microhylids lay their eggs beneath the bark of rotting logs or amongst dead leaves, etc., and the parents may remain with them. In some species the eggs are joined together by a strong thread of mucus, but in others each is separate (although, as in *Eleutherodactylus*, they usually stick together).

Fig. 17 Approximate locations of the occurrence of direct development in frogs. This method is suspected in ten families altogether:

Leiopelmatidae	2 species (New Zealand)
Pelobatidae?	1 species (SE Asia)
Myobatrachidae	3 species (Australia)
Sooglossidae	1 species (Seychelles)
Leptodactylidae	400+ species (Central and South America)
Bufonidae	10 species (South America)
Brachycephalidae?	2 species (Brazil)
Ranidae	60+ species (New Guinea, Solomons, Africa)
Rhacophoridae	4 species (SE Asia)
Microhylidae	100+ species (New Guinea, SE Asia, Africa, South America)

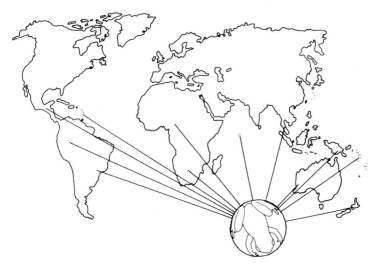

Plate 60   Like all members of its genus, *Eleutherodactylus urichi* lays small clutches of eggs in damp places. The young undergo direct development within the capsule and hatch as tiny fully formed froglets.

Plate 61   A female Surinam toad, *Pipa pipa*, carrying her complement of recently laid eggs. Within one or two days they will have become completely embedded in the swollen skin of her back.

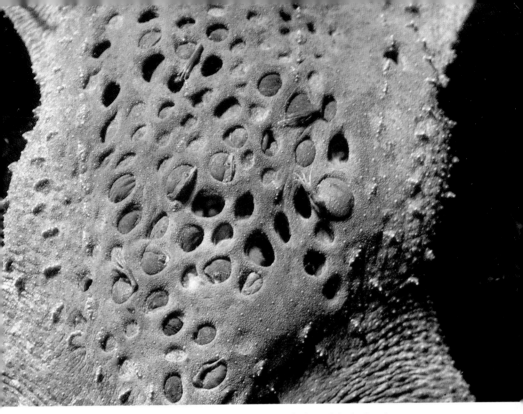

Plate 62   The young Surinam toads, nearing completion of their development, begin to emerge from their cells.

Many other frogs from various families lay terrestrial eggs which undergo direct development, and examples of these and their distribution are pin-pointed on fig. 17. Most have similar breeding habits to the frogs described above and, like them, live in humid environments where terrestrial eggs can survive without water, but *Arenophryne rotunda* is especially interesting. It is a small burrowing frog which inhabits sand dunes in a small part of Western Australia, where substantial rainfall is limited to three or four months of the year. The males call during the rainy season, either from the surface or from a few inches down, and attract mates, but the eggs are not laid for another five or six months. During this time the pair stays in contact under the ground, gradually moving deeper beneath the surface as the upper layers dry out. The eggs, numbering six to twelve, are eventually laid, up to one metre down, at the beginning of the next rainy season and hatch two to three months later when it is well under way. In this way the young frogs have the maximum possible time in which to feed actively before they need to dig themselves in for their first dry season.

2) Eggs carried on back of female

The breeding methods of certain species of *Pipa* toads and marsupial frogs have already been described – they carry their eggs until they have hatched and then release the tadpoles into water. Other species of these frogs, however, retain the eggs until they have developed into fully formed young inside the capsule.

The female Surinam toad, *Pipa pipa*, carries about 100 eggs (plate 61) for a period of approximately 100 days, each in an individual cell. Towards the end of their 'gestation' the young toads may poke various parts of their anatomy out into the water, until they are ready to live independent lives, when they swim away, their release often coinciding with the female shedding her skin.

Of the marsupial frogs, members of five genera carry eggs which undergo direct development. These are:

Cryptobatrachus (three species)
Stefania (six species)
Hemiphractus (five species)
Amphignathodon (one species)
Gastrotheca (twenty-four species)

(But note that eleven other species of *Gastrotheca* release their young as tadpoles – page 117.)

In members of the first three genera, the clusters of eggs merely stick to the dorsal skin of the female, but in the others they are enclosed in a pouch (true 'marsupial frogs'). In some of these species the female may help the young to emerge by flexing her body or even by using her back feet to scoop them out (as in the case of species releasing their young as tadpoles), but in other species the young just hop out when they are ready.

Eggs retained in oviduct of mother

The evolutionary trend towards independence of water reaches its peak in five species of frogs in which fertilisation is internal and is followed by the retention of the developing embryos in their mother's oviduct.

1) Ovo-viviparity

Three of these species are ovo-viviparous – in other words, the oviduct acts as a receptacle for the eggs, replacing (and improving on) the damp moss or leaf-litter in which terrestrial frogs usually lay their eggs. *Nectophrynoides tornieri* and *N. viviparus*, both small bufonids from Africa, and *Eleutherodactylus jasperi*, a leptodactylid from Puerto Rico, produce eggs which undergo direct development inside the female, sustained by their large yolk reserves. *E. jasperi* has a clutch size of three to six eggs and a development time of about 33 days, and the occurrence of ovo-viviparity in this species, only discovered in 1976, leads to speculation as to whether any of the other 400 members of this genus share this habit.

2) Viviparity

Two other species of *Nectophrynoides*, *N. liberiensis* and *N. occidentalis*, are truly viviparous – the young live in the mother's uterus and feed on a substance ('uterine milk') secreted by the epithelial cells which line it. *N. occidentalis*, which is the most extensively studied of the two species, gives birth to 4–35 young toads after a gestation period of about 270 days. For much of this time the female is in aestivation and development is arrested by the production of a hormone, progesterone, from her ovary.

Parental care

Although the careful choice of an egg-laying site or breeding season may be regarded as a form of parental care, the term usually implies some sort of attendance at the egg-clutch or larvae during the incubation and development, either as protection against predators or in order to minimise the effects of an unfavourable environment.

Parental care is closely linked to the reproductive methods described – as frogs have evolved breeding habits in which water is not necessary, so, usually, one or other of the parents invest more time and energy in caring for the eggs or tadpoles. There is also a tendency for clutches to get smaller: *Bufo marinus* lays up to 30,000 aquatic eggs which are left to the mercies of environment and predators, whereas the poison dart frog *Dendrobates pumilio* produces only 4–6 terrestrial eggs at a time but does everything possible to make sure that they survive.

What makes some frogs become more responsible parents than others?

(a) Terrestrial breeding provides more opportunities for guarding the eggs or young, although *Leptodactylus ocellatus* is a notable exception to this; the female (or, sometimes, male) herds the tadpoles together into a tight shoal and drives off potential predators. Otherwise, the best examples of parental care involve species which spawn away from water.

(b) Most 'good' parents are small – they are unable to produce vast quantities of eggs and must therefore try to make each one count.

(c) Many species live in environments which do not provide sufficient conventional breeding sites – examples are rain forests and mountainsides, where surface water soaks away or runs off rapidly. In order to exploit these niches, frogs must find alternative breeding sites and then ensure that the eggs do not dry out or get eaten.

A large number of species protect their eggs by crouching over or near them – in some species, e.g. the Madagascan microhylids, it has been found impossible to prevent the eggs from becoming attacked by mould if the brooding parent is removed, and it seems that the mucus secreted by the adult helps to prevent infection. Other species, e.g. *Centrolenella valerioi*, which sits near its eggs, laid on a leaf overhanging a stream, probably prevent fly larvae from parasitising the eggs by eating or discouraging the adult flies.

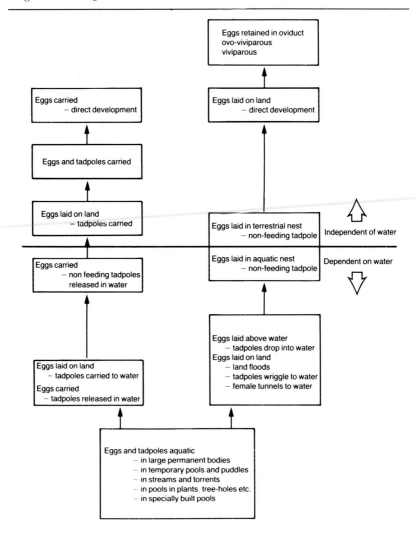

This diagram summarises all of the known breeding methods of frogs and toads, and also charts a possible pathway for the trend leading away from typical aquatic breeding (bottom) and towards viviparity (top). All of the boxes above the horizontal line represent methods in which breeding occurs without water.

A completely different strategy is used by other species, in which one or the other of the parents carries the eggs, tadpoles, or both. It is quite astonishing how many unrelated frogs do this, using a variety of ways in which to achieve it:

a) Eggs wrapped around back legs: *Alytes*
b) Eggs stuck to back: *Hemiphractus, Stefania, Cryptobatrachus, Fritziana*
c) Tadpoles stuck to back: *Sooglossus seychellensis*
d) Eggs in cells on back: *Pipa*
e) Eggs in pouch on back: *Flectonotus, Gastrotheca*
f) Tadpoles in pouches in groin: *Assa*
g) Tadpoles in vocal sac: *Rhinoderma darwini*
h) Eggs (?) and tadpoles in stomach: *Rheobatrachus*
i) Eggs and tadpoles in oviduct: *Nectophrynoides, Eleutherodactylus jasperi*

By moving about, these species are able to maintain favourable conditions for their offspring and prevent them from being eaten (unless they themselves get eaten!).

Between these extremes are species which lay eggs on the ground and then move their tadpoles to more favourable sites (i.e. water) once they have hatched, e.g. the dendrobatids, *Rhinoderma rufum* and perhaps *Leiopelma hochstetteri*; or help them to find their own way there, e.g. *Hyperolius obstetricans*, in which the female kicks her newly-hatched tadpoles into the water from the leaf on which the eggs were laid; or *Hemisus marmoratum*, where the female digs a tunnel from the nest chamber to the bank of a pond.

Although about one species in ten practises parental care in one form or another, the vast majority of these restrict their activities to guarding eggs and/or larvae from predation, infection or desiccation. A small number, however, go one step further and also contribute nourishment to the developing embryo. This is achieved in different ways:

1) Female *Dendrobates histrionicus, lehmanni* and *pumilio* and possibly some other dendrobatids, feed their free-living tadpoles by visiting each one independently and laying infertile 'food eggs' on which it feeds – some rhacophorids and hylids which breed in tree-holes or arboreal plants may have similar systems.

2) Female *Nectophrynoides liberiensis* and *occidentalis* retain their eggs in their oviducts subsequent to internal fertilisation and secrete nutritive proteins on which the developing tadpoles feed.

3) Male *Rhinoderma darwini* appear to produce a similar substance from the cells lining their vocal sac, in which the tadpoles develop.

Chapter 9
Distribution and Movement

Frogs are not equally distributed throughout the world but are restricted by climate and habitat and Chapters 2 and 3 described some of the ways in which morphological, physiological and behavioural adaptations have been forced on frogs to enable them to live in a variety of environments. The physical factors affecting environment are temperature and humidity, i.e. hot or cold, moist or dry. From the numbers of frogs found there we can assume that hot, moist environments suit them best and that cold, dry environments are the least favourable. Superimposed on this principle are factors affecting the dispersal of species and individuals from one region to another – even ideal environments will be poor in frogs if they have had no means of getting there.

Therefore, in order to understand the jigsaw puzzle which comprises the overlapping and interlocking ranges of species and families, it is necessary to study both their habitat requirements and their dispersal and speciation.

Habitat

Very simply, frog habitats are the product of three parameters: temperature, rainfall and topography. Various proportions of each of these ingredients offer a huge array of habitats differing slightly from one another, but for our purposes it is sufficient to look at the most important broad categories.

Lakes

Surprisingly few species are to be found in large bodies of waters, mainly because few frogs or toads are totally aquatic. Notable exceptions are *Xenopus* species in Africa, the Lake Titicaca frog, *Telmatobius culeus*, and a few of its close relatives in South America and a strange bufonid, *Pseudobufo subasper*, in South East Asia.

Aquatic frogs usually have large, heavily webbed hind feet, and their eyes and nostrils are positioned on top of their head. Most are dull grey or brown in colour.

Swamps and marshes

Swamps and marshes are heavily utilised by a variety of frogs. Typically, these species live and forage around the margins, often clinging to reeds and other emergent vegetation, and may enter the water as a ready means of escape from predators.

This is a generalised habitat and a variety of morphological types use it. Apart from those species which lay their eggs in water, a number spawn on overhanging vegetation.

Rivers and streams

Numerous frogs and toads live alongside moving water, benefiting from constantly high humidity levels as well as a ready means of escape. Torrents and waterfalls are utilised by specialised species from a variety of families, e.g. *Heleophryne* species, *Ascaphus truei*, *Amolops* species and *Trichobatrachus robustus*, while many ranids and leptodactylids live along slower-moving watercourses. Centrolenid frogs spawn on leaves overhanging streams; other species spawn in quiet backwaters, spray-pools or attach their eggs to submerged rocks and stones.

Species which live in fast-flowing water have expanded discs on their digits and powerful hind limbs with heavily webbed feet. Adaptation to this environment is most obvious in their tadpoles, which have an enlarged mouth which acts as a sucker, and may have an additional abdominal sucker. One species, *Ascaphus truei*, has internal fertilisation.

Forests

Forests, especially in the tropics, provide many micro-habitats, from the upper canopy where many arboreal species live and breed, down to ground level where a variety of species live amongst the leaf-litter or in burrows beneath the surface. Although forests are rich, both in species and in individuals, this is one of the most difficult habitats to sample due to the ease with which forest species are able to hide and camouflage themselves, and forest communities are amongst the least known.

Because of the number of different micro-habitats, forest species show a wide range of adaptations. Most obvious among these are the ones associated with an arboreal life-style – long legs and adhesive toe-pads. In a few species, e.g. some hylids and rhacophorids, the hands and feet are heavily webbed and are used for gliding. A number of arboreal species breed above the ground in pools of water which collect in plants and tree-holes. Many are green in colour but others are grey or brown, while some imitate lichens, etc. Several have flash markings, usually in the groin region. Forest floor inhabitants are usually brown in colour and several are cryptically shaped and marked in order to blend in with fallen leaves, etc. Those which live beneath the surface are adapted for burrowing and either have hard tubercles on their hind feet or pointed snouts, reinforced skulls and strong front limbs.

Grasslands

Open country is found mainly in temperate regions or at high altitudes

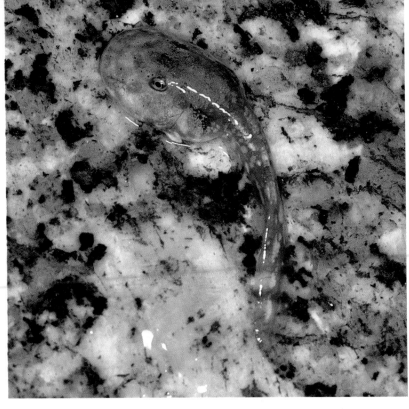

Plate 63   The tadpole of *Amolops* has a large mouth and an abdominal sucker with which it clings to mid-stream boulders (see plate 65) while feeding on bacteria and algae in the spray zone.

Plate 64   The newly emerged *Amolops* has large adhesive toe-pads, similar to those of tree frogs.

Plate 65   A fast-flowing river in Malaysia, the habitat of the specialised ranid
Amolops larutensis.

in the tropics, and climate is therefore a limitation. However, some species are found here, notably ranids and bufonids in Europe and North America, and specialised groups of species in the tropics.

Grasslands are a generalised habitat and no obvious adaptations occur except in the species which live in grassland and moorland at high altitude. These are often dark in coloration and have short limbs and a stout body – a form which lends itself to cold climates.

Mountains

Again, climate can be a limitation at high altitude, but the main problem in mountains is a lack of standing water in which to breed. Forested slopes, especially cloud forests, provide habitats for arboreal species, many of which breed without the need for water, e.g. by laying eggs which develop directly or which are carried on the female's back. Screes and rock faces are inhabited by small numbers of species such as *Leiopelma* species, *Syrrhopus* species and *Alytes mulatensis*, most of which also breed without the need for standing water. Once again, the terrain makes sampling difficult.

Deserts

Total deserts are inhospitable places for animals with permeable skins, but arid regions in many parts of the world are inhabited by species which have evolved life-styles which enable them to survive long periods of drought.

Species from dry environments show a number of interesting adaptations. Most burrow, and some, such as *Scaphiopus* and *Notaden* species have a horny 'spade' on their hind feet and shuffle backwards into the ground. Others, such as *Arenophryne rotunda* (which lives in sand dunes), go down head first, using first their snout and then their front limbs to push their way through the substrate. Very many species are able to remain underground for long spells by virtue of their shape – round bodies and short limbs – which reduces evaporation, and by forming a specialised cocoon, consisting of several layers of sloughed skin, which enables them to retain moisture. They rarely have a well-defined breeding season, but spawn opportunistically when temporary pools form after heavy rain. Most species are yellow, yellowish brown or reddish, according to the soil type in which they live.

At least two arboreal species, *Phyllomedusa sauvagei* and *Chiromantis xerampelina*, from Patagonia and Africa respectively, live in arid regions. They adapt by coating their skin with a waxy secretion to avoid desiccation and both species also save water by excreting their waste-products in the form of semi-solid urea.

Movement and distribution

Although they are less mobile than many other groups of animals, frogs

Plate 66   *Atelopus ignescens*, a specialised inhabitant of high Andean moorland (páramo) up to 4,000 metres. Its dark colour, short limbs and diurnal habit enable it to survive in a cold environment.

and toads do move about. Their movements may be considered on a small scale: the wanderings and migrations of individuals or groups of individuals in search of food, shelter, breeding sites, etc. – or on a larger scale: the movements and dispersal of species and families across the earth's surface.

Home ranges

On an individual level, adult frogs and toads seem to live in a fairly well-defined territory, foraging over a limited area at night (assuming that they are nocturnal) and returning to a known hiding place by morning. These hiding places consist of nooks and crannies in trees, beneath rocks or amongst debris. Tree frogs frequently hide in the leaf axils of plants or, in the New World, in bromeliads. Unusual hiding places include the use of rodent (*Lagostomus maximus*) burrows by several South American species such as *Leptodactylus laticeps* and *L. bufonius*, and of empty snail shells (*Achatina*) by the East African bufonid *Mertensophryne micranotis*.

A number of species use human habitations and artifacts as daytime

133

Plate 67 Amazonian Ecuador. Neo-tropical rain forests have by far the richest frog fauna, both in terms of numbers of individuals and species. The Andean foothills in the distance are covered with cloud forest (montane rain forest) which provides additional types of habitat for yet more species.

Plate 68 An important difference between tropical rain forests in the New and Old Worlds is the proliferation of bromeliad plants in the former. These epiphytes collect water in their central 'vases' and provide hiding places as well as breeding sites for a wide variety of species.

Plate 69   Small streams provide breeding sites for numerous species which live
in surrounding rain forest, in this case, South East Asia.

hiding places. These range from the familiar toad in the greenhouse to species which are rarely if ever found away from human settlements, for instance *Kaloula pulchra* and *Bufo melanostictus* in South East Asia. During spells of dry weather in tropical regions, members of the Hylidae are also liable to take up residence in bathrooms and showers, no doubt attracted by the cool damp atmosphere, and at least one new species, *Litoria splendida*, was first described from a specimen found on the floor of a hotel ablution block in Australia!

There are many reports of distinctively marked frogs and toads which take up residence in a certain place and can be reliably found there day after day – sometimes year after year. The area over which an individual operates is known as its home range and may consist of a few square metres or many hundreds. In some cases, the home range may include a breeding site, but most individuals must make periodic excursions outside their home ranges in order to breed. These are known as migrations and are well documented for many temperate species, and also undoubtedly occur for tropical ones. Migrating animals move towards suitable breeding sites when conditions are right, often being found on the very same leaf or in the same part of a pond as during previous bouts of breeding.

The means by which these animals find their way to a known breeding site and then back to their home range is not completely understood but many, those which do not have far to go, probably navigate largely by memory – this is not difficult to understand, as humans do it every time they go shopping. Migrations over longer distances (similar to those which we make when we go on holiday) probably involve other navigational aids. Breeding animals may be attracted by the chorus of males already there – perhaps the first ones to arrive didn't have far to go. Then again, many probably head downhill, perhaps homing in on a trail of gradually increasing humidity, or on the scent of algae. It has been shown that some species are capable of celestial or solar navigation, a process which necessitates a fairly sophisticated in-built clock in order to allow for the changing position of the sun and stars throughout the year. All in all, frogs and toads are pretty good at finding their way about – individuals which have been deliberately moved away from their home range have usually returned, often before their investigator has. One aspect about which we know very little, however, concerns the dispersal of newly metamorphosed animals: although it is popularly believed that frogs always return to the pond in which they originated, there is, as yet, little or no evidence to support this.

Zoogeography

The dispersal of species and families throughout the world is an event which belongs to a totally different time-scale but which nevertheless owes its origins to the movements and migrations of individuals. Whole populations of frogs do not suddenly lift their roots and move *en masse*, but gradually change their range over many generations by a continual process of expansion and contraction. During successful periods, populations grow until they become overcrowded and this forces some animals to move into fresh areas. During less successful periods, areas are vacated, but these are not always the most recently populated ones. In this way the range of a population changes almost imperceptibly and often as a result of slowly changing conditions. Some species adapt to new habitats better than others and these become widespread, sometimes at the cost of other, more specialised, species whose ranges may become smaller and smaller until they disappear altogether – the same happens, only much more quickly, when vigorous species are dispersed artificially, i.e. by human introduction (see page 145).

Obviously, species can only spread within the limits imposed by natural barriers – deserts, mountains, oceans, etc. In fact, they spread along areas of suitable habitat, known as dispersal corridors, but over the millions of years during which frogs and toads have been around these barriers and corridors have not always been in the same places. Thus, species from northern Europe were able to spread into the British Isles until a few thousand years ago, when the English Channel was formed, whereas species in South America were not able to move north into Central and North America until fairly recently because the two land-masses were separate.

When the first frogs appeared, nearly 200 million years ago, all of the continents as we now know them (except Europe/Asia) were joined, and dispersal was relatively easy. However, as more families evolved, the land-masses began to drift apart, first east-west, isolating South America, Africa, India and Australia from North America, then into smaller chunks which slid around the globe for 100 million years or so, occasionally bumping into each other or tearing themselves apart. As connections were made, opportunities arose for newly evolved animals to spread to fresh areas: conversely, they ran the risk of being overrun by their new neighbours. Some groups worked their way around the world: South America and Africa, which were joined, separated – at about the same time the eastern part of Africa, later to become Madagascar and India, also drifted away. The animals living on Madagascar remained isolated, but those on the Indian segment were later able to spread to South East Asia and then to Australasia, which was in contact with this segment for a brief period. Thus, successful families like the hylids were carried around the world as passengers on vast drifting islands, moving to adjacent 'islands' as the opportunities arose, and evolving all the while into new forms in order to cope with changing conditions – they quite literally 'leap-frogged' from one continent to another. Other groups were able to hold their ground in the face of changing conditions but were unable to spread but, inevitably, many disappeared, either through their inability to adapt or through competition.

From this (very simplified) account of a chain of events which coincided with the evolution and speciation of frogs, it can be seen that the distribution, or zoogeography, of the 21 families may be accounted for by a number of alternative explanations, bearing in mind that the 3,500 or so living species only represent those that have survived the various evolutionary pressures – the 'state of the art' frogs, to use a modern term.

The distribution patterns of the surviving frog families can be categorised as follows:

1) *Relict families.* These arose when land-masses were joined, and were formerly widespread, but now have only isolated pockets of species remaining, the others having become extinct.
   Example: Leiopelmatidae.
2) *'Southern families'.* These colonised the southern continents but failed to move north when the land-masses re-joined.
   Example: Pipidae.
3) *'Northern families'.* These colonised the northern land-mass (Europe/Asia) but failed to spread south.
   Example: Discoglossidae, Pelobatidae.
4) *Cosmopolitan families.* These arose in various places and then exploited continental movements to spread to many parts of the world.
   Example: Bufonidae, Hylidae, Ranidae.
5) *Isolated families.* These arose in isolated areas, especially islands, and were therefore unable to spread, or they have evolved recently.
   Example: Sooglossidae (Seychelles), Heleophrynidae (southern Africa), Rhinodermatidae (extreme southern South America).

By dividing the world up into its zoogeographical regions (fig. 18) it is possible to construct a kind of 'league table' showing the relative richness and diversity of frog families in each:

1) *Neotropical* (Central and South America)
   By far the richest region, having over one third of all species and genera of frogs. (To put this into perspective, Ecuador, one of the

Fig. 18   Zoogeographic regions of the world.

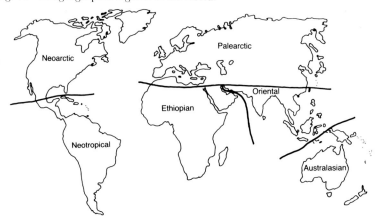

smallest South American countries, had 317 species of frogs recorded up to 1982 – 118 of these had been described since 1970 and so this tally will certainly have grown by now. Britain, which is only slightly smaller, has three native species, and the United States, infinitely bigger, has just over eighty.) Twelve of the twenty-one families are present, including five which are endemic (Brachycephalidae, Rhinodermatidae, Pseudidae, Centrolenidae and Dendrobatidae) and two more which only just reach up into North America (Rhinophrynidae and Leptodactylidae). In addition, the families Bufonidae, Leptodactylidae and Hylidae are represented here by large numbers of enormously diverse species. In contrast, the Ranidae is represented by only a single species (*Rana palmipes*).

2) *Ethiopean* (Africa, except the Mediterranean region)
Eight families are present, including three which are endemic (Heleophrynidae, Hyperoliidae and Sooglossidae), of which the Hyperoliidae shows the greatest diversity. The Ranidae and Bufonidae are well represented, as is the Microhylidae, especially on Madagascar.

3) *Oriental* (South and South East Asia)
Seven families are present, but none are endemic. A high degree of diversification is shown by the Rhacophoridae, Ranidae, Pelobatidae and Microhylidae.

4) *Neoarctic* (North America)
Seven families are present, of which two only just reach the region from South America. There are no endemic families.

5) *Palearctic* (Europe, northern Asia, Mediterranean region of Africa)
Six families are present of which one, the Pelodytidae, is endemic.

6) *Australasia* (Australia, New Zealand and New Guinea)
Four families are present, including one, the Myobatrachidae, which is endemic. Three of the four species belonging to the Leiopelmatidae are found in New Zealand (the other occurs in North America), where they are the only native frogs. There is an enormous diversity of forms and life-styles amongst the Myobatrachidae, Microhylidae and Hylidae (which are sometimes considered as a separate family, the Pelodryadidae).

Chapter 10
Frogs and Man

An animal which changes from an aquatic, fish-like larva to a four-legged land creature, which appears in large numbers following, and sometimes preceding, rain, and which vocalises in varied and often weird ways during the night is an obvious candidate for the starring role in ancient myths and legends. Furthermore, its bulging eyes and vaguely human shape endear it to cartoonists and writers of fairy stories, while its convenient size, interesting life-history and availability make it ideal cannon-fodder for the biology student. It is also edible (and rarely bites back) and has the questionable virtue of being able to predict childbirth in humans; no wonder then that the frog (or toad) has a history which has often touched on that of the human species, and that many civilisations have, at various times, wondered at, exploited, revered, eaten and loathed it.

Legends and folklore

In the ancient civilisations – the Egyptians, Chinese, and the Central Americans, for instance – frogs go back a long way. The Egyptians believed that a frog-headed goddess, Heket, together with her husband, Khnumu (who had a goat's head) engineered the creation of men and other gods, and the hieroglyphic symbol of Heket was a frog, while the number 100,000 was represented by a tadpole, presumably owing to their abundance at certain times of the year. Their most widely read encounter with man, however, occurred around 1000 BC in the city of Rameses where, the Bible tells us, a plague of frogs served as the second in a series of ten disasters brought about as a result of the unreasonable behaviour of the Pharaoh. It seems likely that this legend was based on a particularly successful breeding season, culminating in exceptional numbers of frogs metamorphosing and spreading out over the surrounding countryside. (The subsequent plagues of insects and disease may well have come about as a result of most of these frogs failing to find sufficient food, dying, and decomposing rapidly and odorously during the hot North African summer.)

Frogs were also familiar to the Chinese and Indians, who believed that the world rested upon the back of a gigantic example, and that earthquakes and tremors were the result of his slightest movement. Another belief was that eclipses of the moon were caused by a frog (or toad – the Chinese did not distinguish between the two) swallowing it. This individual, known by two names, Hsia ma or Chan-chu, possessed only

Plate 70   Stylised frogs often figure in traditional designs, such as in this tapestry from Saquilisi in Ecuador.

three legs and was the local counterpart to our 'man in the moon'. Many Chinese legends involved frogs and they also figure as subjects for pottery decoration and carving, both in China and Japan, where their rotund shape, as well as their legendary associations, must have made them eminently suitable models for netsuke carving.

In Central America, the Maya Indians regarded the frog as a consort of the god Chac. Chac was responsible for the coming of the rain and the frog Uo calls loudly when it is time for Chac to sprinkle the earth with water from his gourd. Through their association with water, frogs are linked not only with the growth of crops, but also with fertility and birth, and the tadpole, as well as the adult version, was frequently incorporated into the design of pots, clothing, ornaments and furniture, while stone or pottery effigies were often buried with the dead.

Moving rapidly forward to the Middle Ages, frogs and toads began to take on more sinister roles in Europe. They became associated with evil and witchcraft, often being cited, alongside black cats and the like, as witches' familiars, and also figuring in recipes for various brews and potions. The toad's one saving grace was that it was believed that a precious stone was embedded in its head. These stones, known logically as 'toadstones', were credited with a number of magical powers including the detection and neutralisation of poisons, and the curing of all kinds of stomach aches and cramps. Many techniques were suggested for obtaining one of these stones and any number of unusual minerals were marketed on the pretext of being the genuine article. Even William Shakespeare's 'Duke Senior' appears to have been taken in by the legend: 'Sweet are the uses of adversity; Which, like the toad, ugly and venomous; Wears yet a precious jewel in his head.' (*As You Like It*, Act 2, scene i)

Earlier this century, Kenneth Grahame redressed the balance slightly in his children's story *The Wind in the Willows* in which the character 'Toad' is portrayed as a roguish, pompous, but nevertheless likeable fellow. On the other hand, other stories tell of witches changing handsome princes into toads which can only revert back to their more acceptable form as the result of a maiden's kiss – a form of metamorphosis which has yet to be proved scientifically!

Despite the passing of several hundred years, and the 'Age of Enlightenment', it is still widely maintained that handling toads will cause warts, while the sight of a toad is often the cause of revulsion in otherwise rational people.

The frog, in an entirely different way, has hardly fared any better. Far from being loathed, it has become a widely accepted item of food, not only in France, the land of the frog, but also in many other parts of the world. The species eaten in Europe is *Rana esculenta*, known, aptly, as the edible frog, and in Asia a number of species end up in the wok, including *Rana tigrina*, *Rana crancivora* and *Rana macrodon*. In the West Indies, *Leptodactylus pentadactylus* may be served up as 'mountain chicken'. This book is not the place to give recipes for frog dishes, but it is worth noting that it is usually only the legs which are grilled, fried, boiled or turned into soup. Attempts to produce 'super-frogs' by crossing the large American bullfrog, *Rana catesbeiana*, with tastier species have been tried and abandoned in various places, as have attempts to introduce this species into parts of Jamaica and Cuba as a source of protein. Among more 'primitive' civilisations, a number of native peoples are known to include

Plate 71   *Rana esculenta*, the French gourmet's best-known victim.

frogs in their diet, and why not? Judging from the amount of effort which is required in order to catch some of these leaping, swimming and diving species it seems doubtful if more than a very small proportion meet their end in this fashion (or that the nutritional value of the end product goes very far towards matching the energy expended in obtaining it).

In Australia, some of the desert-dwelling species, notably the water-holding frog, *Cyclorana platycephalus*, are used by aborigines as a source of water – when squeezed they yield a surprisingly large quantity of (allegedly) pure water from their bladders.

In many parts of the western world, however, the frog is more familiar, not on the dining table but on the dissecting table. Hundreds of thousands of frogs, mainly *Rana temporaria* and *Rana pipiens*, donate their bodies, albeit unwillingly, to the cause of science and education – this is rarely in the name of herpetology but as part of a course in comparative physiology and anatomy: the frog is slotted in between a fish and rat, with sometimes a lizard to keep it company. In research, frogs are used, in smaller numbers, for more specific investigations. Attempts are being made, for example, to encourage the celebrated stomach-brooding frog (see page 120) to give up the secret of its ability to inhibit the secretion of digestive juices for the duration of its 'pregnancy' in the hope that ulcer sufferers may be able to benefit. Not so many years ago the ability of the

143

Plate 72   In Asia, several large ranids, including *Rana macrodon*, are regularly
eaten.

African clawed toad, *Xenopus laevis*, to lay eggs spontaneously when
injected with human chorionic gonadotrophin (a hormone which is present in the urine of pregnant women) was used as a means of pregnancy
testing, and many hospitals held large stocks of this common aquatic
species. (In fact, many species of frogs and toads would have been
equally suitable: *Xenopus* was widely used because it was common, cheap
and easily maintained.) More recent techniques using simple chemical
tests have replaced the use of toads, although the same species is still
widely used in teaching and research.

Perhaps the most unusual use of frogs by man concerns the so-called
poison dart frogs of the family Dendrobatidae. Several species of this
South American family secrete powerful toxins from glands in their skin
(see Chapter 4) and three of them, *Phyllobates aurotaenia*, *P. bicolor* (plate
38) and *P. terribilis*, are used by groups of Choco Indians living in the
forests of western Colombia to supply the poison with which they anoint
their blowpipe darts. The way in which they do this depends on the
species being used. *P. aurotaenia* and *P. bicolor* are skewered on a stick and
may be warmed over a fire to induce them to secrete a large quantity of
their poison, but *P. terribilis* is so toxic that only small amounts of its skin
secretions are required, and it is merely pinned to the ground with a
stick (handling it can cause severe irritation). The darts, which are
fashioned from slivers of wood from a palm stem, are etched with a

144

Plate 73 African clawed toads, *Xenopus laevis*, were once widely used in hospital laboratories for pregnancy testing.

spirally arranged groove for the first inch or so of their length, and the poison collects here when the tip of the dart is wiped or rolled across the frog's back. Once the poison has dried, the darts retain their potency for up to one year, and are used to hunt birds and mammals, and may formerly have been used in warfare.

Another dendrobatid species, *Dendrobates tinctorius*, is claimed to have been used for other, more peaceful, purposes – Indians in parts of the Amazon basin were thought to use secretions of this frog to dye the feathers of parrots from green to yellow or red. However, although this story is often repeated, and the species is commonly known as the 'dyeing poison dart frog', this practice appears not to have been reliably substantiated.

Sometimes, attempts to harness frog-power backfire. The large South American toad *Bufo marinus* was used in the nineteenth century to control pests of sugar cane in the West Indies and Puerto Rico and was introduced later into Hawaii and the Philippines. Results of these introductions were watched with no small amount of interest in other cane-growing countries, not least Australia, and the decision to release them in Queensland was made in 1935. Despite certain misgivings and warnings, 62,000 captive-bred toadlets were released and they took to their new home with such enthusiasm that within a few years parts of the state were alive with them. So far, so good, but surveys carried out in

145

Plate 74   The globe-trotting marine, giant or cane toad, *Bufo marinus*.

Plate 75   An *Eleutherodactylus* frog which travelled over 4,000 miles in a bunch of bananas. Small frogs are easily transported inadvertently in tropical produce and may extend their ranges in this way.

Plate 76   The Asian painted frog, *Kaloula pulchra*, is closely associated with villages and towns in South East Asia – in fact it is rarely found anywhere else.

subsequent years seemed to show that the toads were not busily engaged in stamping out sugar cane pests, but had spread to many other areas, including residential ones, where they produced the usual, unfavourable, reaction to toads the world over. The matter of their benefits versus their harmful effects will probably never be resolved, the conclusion tending to depend on whether one is for or against toads in general, but considering the appetite of this species for practically anything which moves, coupled with its astronomical reproductive potential (up to 30,000 eggs per spawning) and its apparent lack of any serious predators in Australia, it would certainly be remarkable if the toad was not well on the way towards upsetting the delicate balance of nature in its adopted home, a factor which has prompted authorities in other parts of the country to impose severe restrictions on the importation of this species for any reason whatsoever. One of the few benefits of the exercise has been the ready availability of the animals for dissection in schools and universities, and as a source of income in areas where they are common by re-exportation to other countries.

The main point of the Australian venture has been to highlight the problems associated with the introduction of non-native animals (and plants) without sufficient knowledge of their effects on the local wildlife and ecology. The lesson has spread to many other countries, and species which, like the cane toad, may become established, are outlawed. Sometimes these have come too late, however, as experiences with *Xenopus laevis* in certain river systems in the United States have shown, while *Rana catesbeiana*, introduced into the San Joaquin Valley, California, eliminated *Rana aurora* and reduced the population of *R. boylii* in the area.

Of course, not all frog introductions are deliberate. As man moves goods and agricultural products around the world it is inevitable that frogs will inadvertently hitch a ride. A frequent stowaway is the tree frog *Ololygon rubra*, a little brown and cream striped frog common in Central and South America and parts of the West Indies, which has a weakness for bananas – not for eating them but for hiding amongst them. Because of this it often turns up in fruit stores in England and, presumably, elsewhere. Being a tropical species it would not be able to establish itself in cooler countries but it seems reasonable to assume that now and again it finds itself somewhere favourable and may survive and even establish itself.

Frogs and toads also find themselves in foreign parts as a result of a growing interest in more unusual pets. This involves a relatively small number of species, mainly those which are common in areas where collectors operate and which are adaptable enough to tolerate confinement. Species such as *Hyla cinerea*, the green tree frog of North America, and *Bufo marinus*, the globetrotting cane toad, form the 'bread and butter' of this trade, and there is a limited but steady market for a large variety of the more exotic species such as the poison dart frogs, horned toads, *Ceratophrys* and *Megophrys* species, African bullfrog, *Pyxicephalus adspersus*, and the Asian tree frog, *Polypedates leucomystax*. Generally speaking, the demand is met by collecting from wild populations, but a few species are regularly bred in captivity, giving numerous advantages: offspring are normally free from disease and parasite infestation; they tend to adapt to captivity better; both males and females are available (wild-caught individuals are predominantly males, which are easier to find due to their vocalisations); and some species are no longer legally obtainable from their country of origin.

The subject of collecting frogs for the pet trade is controversial. A number of countries now prohibit the exportation of frogs along with other animals as a conservation measure, and, while this is very commendable, it is a curious paradox that several of these very countries have the worst records when it comes to a far more serious threat – that of habitat destruction. Enormous areas of rain forest in South America and South East Asia are being indiscriminately logged out or cleared for small-scale agriculture, producing a devastating and irreversible effect on all aspects of plant and animal communities. Unfortunately, many of these areas have not been well enough studied to know which species occur there and many interesting forms are undoubtedly being exterminated before their existence is even recognised. For example, the small green tree frog, *Rhacophorus smaragdinus*, was discovered in 1983 in Taiwan. Its complete range is within a small valley already ear-marked for flooding due to the construction of a dam on the Feitsui River. The even more sudden rise and fall of the gastric brooding frog, *Rheobatrachus silus*, is documented on page 120 – how many other doomed species go unnoticed in huge land-clearance programmes and development projects throughout the world? In temperate regions, frogs and toads are little better off. As land is drained for agriculture their breeding sites disappear, those which are left are often polluted by industrial effluent, and even sites far away from development may be affected by atmospheric pollution, which now crosses geographical and political barriers. The adult animals, feeding as they do on insects, are deprived of food as the use of pesticides becomes more widespread and, as if this were not enough, huge numbers of them are destroyed on the roads as they make their way to spawning ponds. The frog's main problem is that by virtue of its life-history it requires two distinct habitats – land and water – and the destruction or pollution of either one will eliminate it from that area. This is exacerbated by its limited mobility, making it almost impossible for re-colonisation to take place in areas from which it has been ousted, or for it to move away from threatened areas and into more favourable ones. Regrettably, frogs do not provoke the same response as some other types of threatened animals and very few are protected *per se*, and yet, because of their susceptibility to environmental change and disturbance, they are probably amongst the most important indicators of these conditions that we have.

Among those which do enjoy total protection are *Bufo houstonensis* in the United States, *Bufo calamita* in Great Britain, *Bufo pereglenes* in Costa Rica and all three species of *Leiopelma* in New Zealand. All of these are extremely restricted in habitat and therefore especially vulnerable. Other species derive protection by being fortunate enough to live in nature reserves or national parks, but their greatest protection by far would be a more rational approach to the exploitation of wild places for agricultural purposes, mineral extraction and so on.

Chapter 11
The Families of Frogs

The purpose of this section is to bring together the species which have been referred to in the thematic chapters and arrange them into some sort of order. Where space permits, points of interest pertaining to species or groups of species are noted and some of these are cross-referenced to other chapters where more detailed information is given.

As in all such accounts, the purpose is to split a large number of species, about 3,500 in this case, into smaller and more manageable units consisting of species which are thought to be closely related, although these groups are not equal in size. Because the divisions between one family and another are somewhat artificial, and because many species are not well known, experts vary in their opinions as to what constitutes a family, but the system used here is that of Duellman and Trueb in their *Biology of Amphibians*, which is the most widely accepted one at the moment.

Leiopelmatidae

Members of this family form the oldest surviving group of frogs. They are assumed to have been widespread in former times (fossils of similar frogs have been found in Argentina) but are now reduced to four species living on opposite sides of the world. They have no eardrums or vocal sacs. One species has a 'tail', the other three have no tails but retain the muscles which would control it if they did have one!

The tailed frog, *Ascaphus truei*, occurs in the north-western corner of the United States and is restricted to cold mountain streams. Its 'tail' is in fact an extension of the cloaca and is found only in the male. He uses it to transfer sperm to the female, for fertilisation is internal – this arrangement ensures that the sperm is not washed away as it would be if it was released into the rapidly flowing water. The eggs are not laid until ten months later and are attached to the underside of stones on the stream bed – the stream-adapted tadpoles take up to three years to complete their development.

The other three members of the family belong to the genus *Leiopelma* and all have small ranges in New Zealand, where they are the only native frogs. Hochstetter's frog, *L. hochstetteri*, is the commonest species and is found near small streams and seepages in several parts of North Island. Its terrestrial eggs hatch into non-feeding tadpoles and there are reports that they may be carried for a while on the back of one of the parents. The other two species have direct development – the froglets

Plate 77   The midwife toad, *Alytes obstetricans*, a small European discoglossid.

hatch from their egg capsules before their tails are completely absorbed. Both live in regions with no free-standing water, *L. archeyi* in the Coromandel Range of North Island and *L. hamiltoni* on Maud Island and Stephens Island in the Cook Straits. *L. hamiltoni* was thought to have been extinct between 1927 and 1950 but was re-discovered in a small pile of rocks on Stephens Island. The Maud Island population was found in 1958. All four of these unusual species are very rare and are legally protected.

Discoglossidae

The Discoglossidae comprises eleven species of various appearances and habits. *Discoglossus* species are known as painted frogs and live in Europe, North Africa and the Middle East. They are normally found near water and lay their eggs in small clumps throughout an extended breeding season. *Barbourula* (2 species) is from the Philippine Islands and is apparently highly aquatic, but its habits are not well known. Frogs of the genus *Bombina* are known collectively as fire-bellied toads due to their brightly coloured ventral surfaces, which may be yellow, orange or red, and which are used in aposematic display.

The two European species, *B. bombina* and *B. variegata*, live in small bodies of water, sometimes temporary puddles and ditches. Their eggs are laid singly onto the bottom, and are produced throughout a long breeding season. All three species of *Alytes* are known as midwife toads. *A. obstetricans* is widespread in Europe whereas *A. cisternasii* has a limited range in Portugal. Males of both species carry their strings of eggs around their hind limbs and release the tadpoles into water. They are secretive toads which live beneath rocks and in burrows, from which the male calls. *Alytes muletensis* is the most recently discovered frog in Europe (in 1977). It escaped notice for so long because it lives in small colonies in crevices in limestone cliffs on the island of Majorca. It too carries its eggs.

Rhinophrynidae

This family contains only one species, the Mexican burrowing toad, *Rhinophrynus dorsalis*, a large rotund species with a pointed snout and short limbs. For a burrowing frog it is quite colourful, with a red or orange dorsal line on a dark background. It lives in Central America, from southern Texas to Costa Rica, but is only found in the drier lowland parts of this region. It lives beneath the ground most of the time, digging itself in with 'spades' on its hind feet, and emerges to breed when heavy rain floods the ground. The males have internal vocal sacs and they call from the surface of the water. The eggs float to the surface and the tadpoles are filter feeders.

Pipidae

The Pipidae consists of twenty-six species of aquatic frogs. Seven, belonging to the genus *Pipa*, live in South America and the others, in three genera, are African. All are highly adapted to an aquatic life-style and have huge, heavily webbed hind feet and powerful hind limbs. Their eyes and nostrils are positioned on the top of their heads, and they are unique in not having tongues.

The *Pipa* species are remarkable for their reproductive habits in which the eggs are embedded on the back of the female (plate 61). They live in still waters of lakes and swamps where their shape and colouring provide good camouflage. Their eyes are small and they appear to hunt mainly by detecting prey with their outstretched fingers. The largest species, the Surinam toad, *Pipa pipa* (plate 13), is greatly flattened in shape, but has a large mouth and a prodigious appetite.

The best-known African genus is *Xenopus*, collectively known as clawed toads. These species are also dull-coloured, although some have brighter undersides. Like *Pipa* species, they typically hang just below the surface with outstretched arms, waiting for food to swim by. Of the fourteen species, *X. laevis* is the most familiar, having been used as a laboratory animal for many years, originally for pregnancy testing and later for anatomical and embryological research. As a result it has found its way into foreign parts and feral colonies now exist in the United States and in Britain. *Xenopus* species lay their eggs singly and they may be attached to aquatic plants, rocks or debris. The tadpoles are filter-feeders. The remaining species, four in *Hymenochirus* and one in *Pseudhymenochirus*, are small species from West Africa. These frogs are dark in colour and feed on aquatic invertebrates and possibly young fishes. The tiny eggs are laid on the surface after an elaborate display of underwater looping and the tadpoles, in *Hymenochirus* at least, are carnivorous.

Pelobatidae

Frogs of this family are commonly known as spadefoot toads, although only two genera, *Scaphiopus* and *Pelobates*, are specialised burrowers. All six species of *Scaphiopus* live in North America, where they are the only representatives of the family. They live in arid regions where they dig themselves into the ground using the flange of hard skin on their back feet which gives them their name. Sporadic rain storms galvanise them into activity and they emerge and spawn over two or three nights, the development of the eggs and tadpoles being completed within two or three weeks. The tadpoles of some species are of two types: herbivores, which eat algae and other plant material; and carnivores, which prey on other tadpoles (see page 67).

The four species of *Pelobates* occur in Europe, North Africa and the Middle East. They are similar to *Scaphiopus* in shape and habits, but their development is not so rapid. *P. fuscus* is known as the garlic frog for the odour which it supposedly gives off if threatened. Both *Scaphiopus* and *Pelobates* are numerous in the areas where they occur but are rarely seen other than at breeding time.

The rest of the family are Asian, occurring from China, through Indo-China and the Malaysian peninsula into Indonesia and the Philippines. *Megophrys nasuta* (plate 22) is famous for its bizarre shape which camouflages it so well on the rain forest floor where it lives. Altogether there are twenty-one species in this genus, all of which have tadpoles which feed from the water's surface by means of their funnel-shaped mouths, with the exception of *M. longipes* which is probably a terrestrial breeder. *Leptobrachium* species, of which there are eleven, are also forest toads. Males of at least three species have a series of horny spines protruding from their upper lips, and *L. hasselti* (plate 80) has bright orange eyes. Members of this genus and two others, *Leptolalax* and *Scutiger*, breed in streams and their tadpoles are adapted to fast-flowing water. The remaining three genera contain a total of six species and are not well known.

Pelodytidae

This family consists of two species. *Pelodytes punctatus* is the parsley frog of Spain and France. This small secretive frog lives amongst dense vegetation and occasionally burrows in damp soil. It breeds in still water, often ditches, and may breed continuously throughout the summer. The eggs are laid in short strings and are wrapped around aquatic vegetation.

Plate 78   *Xenopus tropicalis*, a small clawed toad from tropical Africa.

Plate 79   Couch's spadefoot toad, *Scaphiopus couchi*, a North American pelobatid from semi-arid regions.

Plate 80 *Leptobrachium hasselti* is an Asian pelobatid found in primary and secondary rain forests. Its orange eyes set it apart from the other members of its genus.

Myobatrachidae

This family, which is exclusively Australian, is sometimes considered to be part of the American family Leptodactylidae. It contains a varied assortment of 106 species of frogs adapted to a wide range of habitats, and these are divided into twenty genera, several of which only contain a single species. The largest genera, *Uperoleia* and *Ranidella*, contain eighteen and thirteen species, all of which are small (about 35 mm), plump brown or grey frogs, many recently described. Their habits are not well known and many have limited distributions, with only a small number having been found. They spawn in water. *Limnodynastes* (twelve species) mostly lives in damp marshy places, although one or two species, e.g. *L. spenceri* and *L. ornatus*, live in semi-arid regions and burrow. All spawn in foam nests floating on the surface of open water, and species from dry regions breed opportunistically after rain. *Pseudophryne* (eleven species) are sometimes known as 'toadlets'. They are small stout frogs which have distinctive black and white bellies. Some, notably the Corroboree toadlet, are also brightly marked dorsally, the species in question being black and yellow. *Pseudophryne* species typically live in damp places – bogs, seepages and marshes – and some at least lay their eggs in small damp depressions in areas which later become flooded.

Neobatrachus contains seven species of desert-dwelling burrowing frogs, several of which are remarkably similar to the American spadefoot toads, right down to the 'spade' on their back feet. Like the latter, they lay their eggs in shallow pools following heavy rain and the tadpoles develop rapidly. *Myobatrachus gouldii* is a strange species with a tiny head, an enormous swollen body and small limbs which stick straight out from the sides – it is known as the turtle frog. It lives in dry regions and spends most of the year underground, where it appears to live entirely on termites, and emerges to mate during rain. The eggs are buried and undergo direct development. *Arenophryne rotunda* is similar in habits, but lives amongst sand dunes. Both of these species burrow head first, using first their pointed snouts and then their front limbs to tunnel a metre or more below the surface, where a trace of moisture can be found throughout the year.

Notaden (three species) are also burrowing species and have globular bodies, but they spawn in temporary pools.

Assa darlingtoni is the Australian marsupial frog (see page 119) and *Rheobatrachus* (two species: one possibly extinct) are the gastric brooding frogs (page 120). All three of these species inhabit the moist montane region on the Queensland-New South Wales border. *Rheobatrachus* are totally aquatic in montain streams but *Assa* lives on damp forest floors amongst leaf-litter, etc. *Megistolotis lignarius* is known as the woodworker frog owing to its call. It lives amongst rocks and boulders and its eggs are laid in a foam nest in rock pools. The tadpoles are torrent-adapted. *Heleioporus* (six species) are robust frogs which make foam nests in burrows near streams, while the tadpoles of *Kyarranus* (three species) and *Philoria frosti* are non-feeding. *Mixophyes* (four species) are the largest frogs in the family, up to 100 mm or more, and feed on other frogs as well as insects, etc. *Taudactylus* (five species) live in torrents and are agile and strong swimmers.

Heleophrynidae – Ghost Frogs

The three species comprising this family are all limited to South Africa in distribution. At various times they have been classified with the Leptodactylidae and the Rhacophoridae, but are now recognised as distinct. All live in or near fast-flowing streams in mountainous areas and have well-developed toe-pads for clinging to wet rocks, and heavily webbed back feet for swimming. They range from 35 to 50 mm in size. Males of all species develop nuptial pads which extend along the inside of their fore-arm, and the Cape ghost frog, *Heleophryne purcelli*, also has small spines around the rim of its lower jaw. This species lays large eggs beneath wet stones in shallow backwaters, alongside streams. The torrent-adapted tadpoles are long and flat in shape and have sucker-like mouths.

Sooglossidae

This family contains just three species: *Nesomantis thomasseti*, *Sooglossus gardineri* and *S. seychellensis*. These are small (up to 40 mm) frogs which are largely terrestrial. All come from the Seychelles Islands in the Indian Ocean, and all lay terrestrial eggs – *S. seychellensis* carries its non-feeding tadpoles on its back, and *S. gardineri*'s eggs undergo direct development. Details of *Nesomantis*' reproduction are unknown.

Leptodactylidae

Although not very familiar to most people, this family, with over 700 members, forms an important part of the rich South and Central American frog fauna. In particular, *Eleutherodactylus* is by far the largest genus of frogs, its 400 species accounting for about 10 per cent of all known species. These are small to medium sized frogs, mostly brown in colour, but sometimes green (plate 6), which range from northern Mexico down into Argentina, including the West Indies. They live in a variety of habitats: most are terrestrial, some are arboreal, while others live on cliff faces, often amongst ground bromeliads. The males often have high, whistling calls, and call incessantly from low vegetation, bushes or trees depending on species. As far as is known, all except one species lay terrestrial eggs which undergo direct development, the exception being *E. jasperi*, which is ovo-viviparous, and at least one other species, *E. coqui*, has internal fertilisation. Parents may remain with their eggs, and *E. angelicus* buries them in sand and then stays nearby until they have hatched. These species are often transported amongst produce, plants and soil (as eggs?) and at least one species, *E. planirostris*, has been introduced into the United States (from Cuba) where it has established itself.

A second large genus, *Leptodactylus*, with fifty species, has a similar range to that of *Eleutherodactylus* but its members are larger on average and are more aquatic in habits. Some, e.g. *L. fallax* and *L. pentadactylus*, are big enough to be eaten (by humans), and many occur in dense populations, especially in marshy areas. They are ranid-like in appearance (plate 81), usually brown or tan, long-legged and agile species. All build foam nests, either on water, damp ground or in burrows. Other foam nesters in this family include the thirty-four species of *Physalaemus*, which often breed in temporary puddles or wheel ruts, and most of the twelve species of *Pleurodema*. Members of both genera are small to medium sized and, although most are grey or brown, some species have brighter markings such as eye-spots.

Plate 81 *Leptodactylus mystaceus*, a common medium sized leptodactylid from South America.

Plate 82   The red-spotted toad, *Bufo punctatus* – a North American toad which lives in arid environments.

Plate 83   The European green toad, *Bufo viridis*, is common in a number of habitats in the eastern Mediterranean region.

The twenty-nine species of *Telmatobius* are Andean in distribution and occupy a variety of habitats. *T. culeus* is the weird Lake Titicaca frog (fig. 7): this species and some others are totally aquatic, living in high volcanic lakes or mountain streams, whereas other, mainly smaller, species are semi-terrestrial. *Batrachophrynus macrostomus* from Peru is also aquatic and lives in high lakes – it is the only member of its genus – and *Phrynopus* (sixteen species) contains a group of terrestrial species from similar elevations. *Syrrhopus* (fifteen species) ranges from southern Texas to Guatemala. Several species live amongst screes or in crevices in rocky outcrops and are known as cliff frogs, and *Hylactophryne* (three species) has a similar range and habitat preference. *Caudiverbera caudiverbera* is known as Gray's frog. It comes from southern Chile and is a large and powerful species which feeds largely on other frogs.

The genera *Ceratophrys* and *Lepidobatrachus*, containing six and three species respectively, are sometimes placed in a separate family: the Ceratophryidae. They are all wide-bodied species with enormous mouths and pugnacious dispositions, feeding on small mammals and other frogs as well as insects, etc. They live sedentary lives, lying partially buried in order to ambush prey and some, e.g. *Ceratophrys cornuta*, have fleshy 'horns' over their eyes to disguise their outline. Budgett's frog, *Lepidobatrachus asper*, and its two relatives, *L. laevis* and *L. llanensis*, which inhabit the dry Chaco region of Argentina, aestivate in clay or mud during the dry season and breed opportunistically after heavy rain. *Ceratophrys ornata* (plate 84) has similar habits in the drier parts of its range.

The remaining 150 or so species of leptodactylids are placed in about forty uncommon or little-known genera, many containing only one to three species.

Bufonidae – Toads

The most numerous (over 200 species) and by far the most familiar group of species in this family are contained in the genus *Bufo*. Its members are found almost throughout the world except in the Arctic and Antarctic regions, Madagascar and New Zealand, although the Australian and New Guinean species *Bufo marinus* was introduced by man. All are terrestrial or burrowing species, although a few, e.g. *Bufo asper* (plate 5) are able to climb moderately well. Their habitats range from tropical forests to semi-desert areas and they are well represented in the temperate parts of the world. Many have become familiar commensals of man. Toads are typically heavy-bodied, warty animals with short back legs. Most have prominent parotid glands, and some have additional poison glands on their thighs, e.g. *B. alvarius*. They range in size from 30 mm (the oak toad, *Bufo quercicus*) to 250 mm (Blomberg's toad, *B. blombergi*) but most are about 40–70 mm in length. Nearly all are primarily nocturnal and brown or grey in colour, but several have a light vertebral stripe (plate 83) and some are brightly coloured with green, tan or orange markings. A number, e.g. *B. canorus*, *B. pereglenes*, show sexual dimorphism in their markings. Most temperate and some

Plate 84　Bell's horned toad, *Ceratophrys ornata*, is one of a group of leptodactylids which are remarkable for their large appetites and pugnacious dispositions.

tropical *Bufo* species are explosive breeders – they congregate in large numbers for a short breeding season and lay long strings of eggs, numbering up to many thousands. Most species have a single vocal sac and a loud trilling call but some, e.g. *B. superciliaris*, are practically voiceless.

The other large bufonid species is *Atelopus*, containing forty-three species from Central America to Bolivia. They show a variation in general appearance which correlates with altitude. Lowland species have long legs, narrow bodies, and many are brightly patterned with yellow, orange or red markings and black reticulations (*A. varius zeteki* from Panama is completely orange-yellow in colour). Montane species such as *A. ignescens* (plate 66) and *A. bufoniformis*, are black or dark grey and have stout bodies and short legs – all adaptations to surviving in cold conditions. These species have been found at over 4,000 metres in the Andes of Ecuador, Colombia and Peru, often occurring in enormous numbers. At least some species are remarkable for their extended amplexus, which may last for several months. All *Atelopus* species lay their eggs in streams, some (perhaps all) in short strings attached to the bottom, and the tadpoles are torrent-adapted, with a large oral disc.

Seventeen species of *Ansonia* come from South East Asia. They are small forest species which, like *Atelopus*, spawn in streams and have torrent-adapted tadpoles. *Nectophrynoides* are all from Central Africa and their main interest concerns their reproductive methods: four species lay eggs, two (*N. tornieri* and *N. viviparus*) are ovo-vivaparous and two (*N. liberiensis* and *N. occidentalis*) are viviparous. *Nectophryne* (two species) is also an African genus, at least one of which, *N. afra*, uses small bodies of water in which to lay its eggs which are then guarded by the male. *Mertensophryne micranotis*, from East Africa breeds in tree-holes and has internal fertilisation – its tadpoles have an odd doughnut-shaped structure on the top of their head as do those of another East African species, *Stephopaedes anotis*, which spawns in similar situations. *Pelophryne brevipes*, and perhaps other members of the genus, which contains eight species altogether, from South East Asia, lays its eggs in leaf axils and has been known to use a broken bottle. *Pseudobufo*, which comes from the Malaysian peninsula, Sumatra and Borneo, contains only one species, *P. subasper*, and is unique amongst bufonids in being totally aquatic, living around the margins of large lakes.

Rhamphophryne, containing five species from Central and northern South America, are strange forest toads with long pointed snouts. Few specimens have been found but it seems likely that their eggs undergo direct development. This method of reproduction also occurs in the two species in each of the South American genera *Oreophrynella* and *Osornophryne*, and of the three species of *Dendrophryniscus*, all from northern South America, at least one, *D. brevipollicatus*, lays its eggs in water-filled bromeliad vases. *Melanophryniscus* consists of eight small South American species, some of which have bright orange or crimson hands, feet and bellies. These are used to warn predators of noxious secretions, and the behaviour known as 'Unkenreflex' has been noted in species such as *M. rubiventris* and *M. stelzneri* (page 53). *Crepidophryne epioticus* is an enigmatic species from Costa Rica: it was described in 1875 from a single specimen and then not heard of again until 1959 when four additional specimens turned up. It is small (up to 35 mm) and has dark blue markings on a grey or orange background. Nothing appears to be known of its habits.

The remaining twenty-six species are divided between six little known African and three Asian genera.

Brachycephalidae – Short-headed Toads

This family was included with the Bufonidae until recently and contains only two species. Both come from south-eastern Brazil and are small

Plate 85   *Pseudis paradoxus*, famous for its gigantic tadpoles, is highly aquatic and lives in ponds, lakes and swamps in northern South America.

Plate 86   A large tree frog, *Phrynohyas venulosa*, which has a wide range in Central and South America. Its colour and markings are highly variable: this example's green 'finger-nails' are not typical.

forest species. *Psyllophryne didactyla* is probably the smallest anuran in the world at under 10 mm and, with one other species of toad, shares the distinction of having four, rather than five, digits on its hind limbs. The other species, *Brachycephalus ephippium*, is a small bright orange species. Amplexus in this species, and probably in *Psyllophryne*, is inguinal, and in this differs from almost all bufonids, and it seems likely that the large unpigmented eggs are laid on land and undergo direct development.

Rhinodermatidae – Mouth-brooding Frogs

Two species are assigned to this family. Darwin's frog, *Rhinoderma darwini*, lives in the *Notophagus* (southern beech) forests of southern Chile and Argentina. It is a small (25–30 mm) species with a pointed snout and varies from green to brown in colour. The underside is black with white blotches. Its call is a high-pitched bird-like whistle, and its unique mouth-brooding method of reproduction is described on page 119. The other species, *R. rufum*, is restricted to Chile and does not brood its tadpoles in the same way but carries them to water.

Pseudidae

The Pseudidae contains four species in two genera. All are superficially ranid-like in appearance (plate 85), and all are strictly aquatic, inhabit-

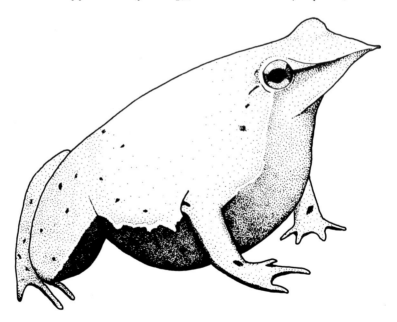

Fig. 19 Darwin's frog, *Rhinoderma darwini*. Males of this species brood tadpoles in their vocal sacs.

ing large swamps and other bodies of still, overgrown water, although they are not entirely helpless on land. *Pseudis paradoxa* is remarkable for the large size of its tadpoles which grow to about three times the length of the adults. This species has an enormous range from the Caribbean coast of Venezuela and Trinidad, right down into Patagonia, and a number of subspecies are recognised. *P. p. platensis* departs radically from the typical life-style by living in seasonally dry regions (Chaco): it gets around this problem by aestivating in mud when its pools dry up. The two species of *Lysapsus* have a composite range taking in southern Brazil, Uraguay, Paraguay and northern Argentina.

Hylidae – Tree Frogs

The hylids comprise 630 species from most of the tropical and sub-tropical parts of the world except Africa. Although this family consists largely of the arboreal 'tree' frogs – climbing species with expanded toe pads – a few species are largely terrestrial and some even burrow.

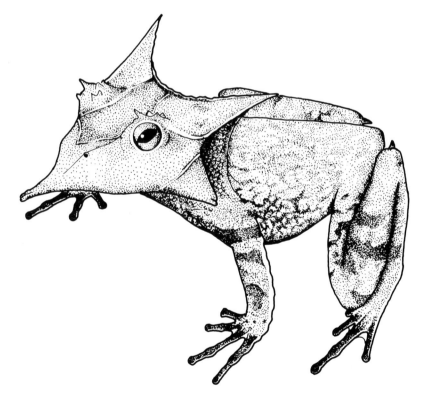

Fig. 20   The world's strangest frogs? The five species of *Hemiphractus* are rare inhabitants of Central and South American rain forests – all carry eggs on their backs, feed mainly on other frogs and may bite if handled.

Plate 87 *Hyla gratiosa*, the barking tree frog of North America, has a call which is remarkably similar to a dog's bark.

Plate 88 *Hyla lanciformis* is a large and agile tree frog from South America. It is one of the few frogs with transverse markings.

Plate 89   Most Australian hylids belong to the genus *Litoria*. White's tree frog, *L. caerulea*, is an unusually large and rotund species which is well adapted to dry environments.

Plate 90   In contrast to the previous plate, *Litoria nasuta* is streamlined, agile and an accomplished leaper. It is appropriately known as the 'rocket frog'.

By far the largest number come from Central and South America. The leaf frogs, genera *Phyllomedusa* (thirty-three species), *Agalychnis* (eight species) and *Pachymedusa* (one species) are large arboreal species, mostly green and often with flash markings in their groin region. Some *Agalychnis* species are notable for their bright red eyes (plate 15). These species are slow-moving and nocturnal in habits and typically breed in bushes and palms, where they attach their eggs to leaves which overhang ponds (page 109). *Phyllomedusa sauvagei* is unusual in coming from dry areas and protects itself from desiccation by wiping a waxy secretion over its skin.

The marsupial frogs comprise fifty-eight species in seven genera. Most carry their tadpoles in pouches on the back of the female, the others carry them in small depressions on their back. The largest genus, *Gastrotheca*, ranges from the humid lowland rain forests of Central and South America to the high inter-Andean plateau at 4,000 metres or more – these highland species are less arboreal than the others and are somewhat toad-like in appearance and habits. The strangest group of marsupial frogs (probably of all frogs) are the five species of *Hemiphractus*. These weird animals have bony triangular heads with long pointed snouts. They live on the forest floor and in low shrubs, but are rarely sighted. They appear to have no voice and females carry their small clutches of eggs in individual depressions on their backs. They probably feed largely on smaller frogs, lizards, etc., and bite fiercely if handled.

Other tropical American genera include *Ololygon*, with fifty-four species, *Phyrnohyas* (five species), members of which secrete a sticky white poison, and *Osteocephalus*, in which the males are warty, females smooth. *Triprion*, with two species, from Mexico, are small frogs with long upturned snouts, and *Pternohyla*, also from Mexico (and southern Arizona), are desert species which burrow. Fourteen other small genera are restricted to South America.

Hyla, the largest genus, with 250 members, occurs mainly in South America, but about twelve species are found in North America, including several well-known ones such as the green tree frog, *H. cinerea*, and the spring peeper, *H. crucifer*, while two, *H. arborea* and *meridionalis*, are found in Europe – the former species also ranges right across Asia and is found in Japan. Most *Hyla* species are arboreal frogs which lay their eggs in small clumps attached to aquatic vegetation in ponds and ditches but some, e.g. *H. rosenbergi*, construct shallow basins at the edge of streams and ponds (plate 52), while others, e.g. *H. leucophyllata*, lay them on overhanging vegetation and some, e.g. *H. zeteki*, breed in bromeliad vases.

Acris and *Pseudacris* (two and seven species respectively) are known as cricket frogs and chorus frogs. They are North American and live in damp and marshy places, hiding amongst vegetation and rarely climbing. They have no toe-pads and are all small (up to 35 mm) brown or green species.

The Australian hylids are sometimes placed in a separate family, the Pelodryadidae. Three genera are recognised. *Litoria* is the largest, with

Plate 91   The Pacific tree frog, *Hyla regilla* of western North America is less arboreal than many of its relatives and usually confines its activities to low shrubs and herbage.

Plate 92 *Dendrobates auratus*, one of the best-known poison dart frogs, comes from Central America.

Plate 93 *Dendrobates tricolor* is a tiny (20 mm) poison dart frog from the Pacific slopes of the Andes in Ecuador.

Plate 94   The genus *Colostethus* contains many small, lively frogs. Although they are related to the poison dart frogs they produce few skin toxins and therefore lack bright markings. This unidentified species comes from western Ecuador.

Plate 95   *Staurois natator*, a torrent-adapted frog from Borneo. Its habit of 'semaphoring' with its back feet, the webbing on which is blue, is a recent observation.

106 species and its members have diversified to fill many ecological niches: several are drought tolerant, e.g. *L. caerulea* and *L. splendida*; others are agile terrestrial species, e.g. *L. nasuta*; but many are arboreal. Most are aquatic breeders but some from New Guinea lay their eggs on overhanging leaves.

Nyctimystes (twenty-six species) is largely New Guinean but three species occur in northern Queensland, Australia. Members of this genus differ from *Litoria* in having vertical pupils – *Litoria* species have horizontal ones. The thirteen species of *Cyclorana* were formerly considered part of the Myobatrachidae but are now recognised as hylids. They are stout frogs with short limbs and they burrow beneath the surface. They are therefore able to live in arid environments and they breed in shallow, often temporary pools – hardly appropriate for members of the 'tree' frog family and undoubtedly the cause of confusion over their classification.

Centrolenidae – Glass Frogs

The Centrolenidae is a family of sixty-five species divided into two unequal genera. *Centrolene geckoideum* is a large (up to 77 mm) species with enormous hands and feet. It lives along streams in the Andean cloud forests of Ecuador and Colombia and lays its eggs on rocks or roots, from which the tadpoles drop into the water.

All the other species are placed in *Centrolenella*. These small (up to 30 mm) delicate frogs are usually green, often flecked with brilliant white or gold, and have transparent skin on their bellies which makes their internal organs visible (hence 'glass' frogs). They live in cloud and rain forests in tropical America, invariably near small forest streams. The eggs are laid on leaves overhanging these streams, into which the tadpoles fall. *C. buckleyi* differs by living above the tree-line – it lays its eggs in large ground bromeliads. All are secretive and many live in inaccessible regions – several new species have been described in recent years, often from just one or two specimens.

Dendrobatidae – Poison Dart Frogs

At present the Dendrobatidae consists of 116 species in three genera. They are small to medium sized frogs (15 mm in *Dendrobates minutus* – 50 mm in *D. tinctorius* and *D. trivittatus*) distributed throughout tropical America. Members of two genera, *Dendrobates* and *Phyllobates*, are remarkable for their brilliant coloration and the associated skin toxins which they produce.

Dendrobatids are inhabitants of tropical rain forests, living colonially on the forest floor, often near small streams. The few species reported from drier areas, e.g. *D. azureus* and *D. bombetes*, are restricted to forest islands or 'inselbergs' within these regions. They are active during the day and are lively foragers amongst the leaf-litter, moving in short hops, rarely still for more than a second or two. Many species have large terminal discs on their digits and climb well in shrubs, mossy tree-trunks, etc., and at least one, *D. arboreus*, is arboreal and lives amongst bromeliads at a height of 15–20 metres above ground level – considering the difficulty in sampling arboreal habitats in tropical forests, it may well be that several more such species await discovery. Food of all species appears to consist mainly of ants and similarly-sized arthropods, and these are snapped up efficiently by the tongue.

The life-history of all dendrobatids, as far as is known, is remarkable. The courtship is elaborate and takes place in a well-defined territory. The eggs are laid on the ground and the tadpoles wriggle onto the back of one of the parents as soon as they hatch. In at least three species, the female deposits each tadpole in a bromeliad vase and 'feeds' it regularly with an infertile egg. A full account is given on page 113.

Because of the great variation in size and colour, the taxonomy of some of the dendrobatids is rather confusing. Furthermore, several species have been variously assigned to *Dendrobates* or *Phyllobates* over the years. It is now generally accepted that *Phyllobates* comprises five species – *aurotaenia*, *bicolor*, *lugubris*, *terribilis* and *vittatus* – and that all the other brightly coloured species, forty-eight in all, belong in *Dendrobates*.

Phyllobates terribilis, discovered in Colombia in 1973, is completely golden-yellow in colour and produces by far the most virulent toxin. *P. bicolor* (plate 38) is similar but has black flecks on its back legs. Amongst the *Dendrobates* species the whole spectrum of colours may be found, often quite astonishing in their brilliance and intensity. It is not possible to describe them all and only a few examples will be given. *D. lehmanni* is boldly banded in red (sometimes yellow) and jet black, *D. auratus* (plate 92) is bronze with blotches of pale metallic green, *tinctorius* is black with blue and yellow stripes and reticulations, and *azureus* is almost completely blue with a few white and black markings. One of the most striking species is *D. reticulatus* (sometimes included with *D. quinquevittatus*): this species has limbs and flanks of black and white in a network arrangement, while the centre of the back and the top of the head are solid bright red.

By comparison, the *Colostethus* species are dingy, but nevertheless interesting for their reproductive behaviour, which follows the usual dendrobatid pattern. Most species are brown, often with a darker dorso-lateral line, and they can be difficult to identify. Their bellies may be mottled black and white or black and pale blue. Males of at least one species, *C. trinitatus*, become darker, almost black, during courtship. In areas where these frogs occur they are often very numerous and their high-pitched chirps and trills are a prominent and evocative part of the forest's sound.

Ranidae

The Ranidae is a large and cosmopolitan family. In addition to the familiar pond frogs, genus *Rana*, it contains forty-six other genera and totals 667 species. The 250-odd species assigned to *Rana* are well distributed throughout the world except in Australia, New Zealand and small

Plate 96 *Rana hosii*, a handsome streamlined frog from South-east Asia.

Plate 97 The golden mantella, *Mantella aurantiaca*, a Madagascan ranid of startling appearance.

Plate 98   A typical reed frog, *Hyperolius tuberilinguis*, from southern Africa. This species also occurs in a plain yellow form.

islands. South America has only one species, *R. palmipes*, but this has a range which covers all but the southernmost part of the continent. Species such as the European common frog, *R. temporaria*, the edible frog, *R. esculenta*, the North American bullfrog, *R. catesbeiana*, and the leopard frog, *R. pipiens*, are the archetypal frogs living around ponds, ditches or in damp gardens and fields and producing large masses of frog-spawn in the spring. Tropical species often differ in their habits and reproductive arrangements: *R. finchi* carry their tadpoles while *R. blythi* and *R. plicatella* spawn in basins specially constructed for the purpose by the males. Most of this genus are long-legged, agile species which are good at jumping, good at swimming and good at surviving – a very successful group of animals.

Other genera may share the same general appearance: thirty-eight species of *Ptychadaena* in Africa and twenty-three species of *Amolops* in Asia, for instance. Others are adapted for burrowing and have 'spades' on their back feet, e.g. *Tompterna* and *Pyxicephalus* from Africa; or pointed snouts, e.g. *Hemisus* from the same continent; and a few are highly aquatic, e.g. *Occidozyga* from Asia; or arboreal – *Platymantis* species from New Guinea and the neighbouring islands. *Amolops* and *Staurois* species from Asia and *Petropedates* and *Strongylopus* species from Africa live in torrents and waterfalls and their tadpoles are adapted accordingly, some having additional abdominal sucker-like discs. At least two of the three species of *Staurois* signal with their bright blue feet, but the function of this behaviour is not fully understood. All species from New Guinea and the Solomon Islands lay large yolky terrestrial eggs which undergo direct development.

Most ranids are grey or brown in colour, and these include the multitude of small and secretive forest species from Central Africa, e.g. *Arthroleptis* and *Phrynobatrachus*, but several are green, e.g. *Rana hosii* (plate 96) from Asia and *R. clamitans* from North America. A few, most notably *Mantella aurantiaca* from Madagascar, are brightly coloured. Most are within the size range 40–80 mm but *Conraua goliath* from West Africa is the world's largest frog at 300 mm or more, while *Microbatrachella capensis* from southern Africa measures only about 15 mm and the five *Cacosternum* species from the same region are little bigger.

Hyperoliidae

With one exception, this family is restricted to Africa and Madagascar, the exception being *Tachycnemis seychellensis* which occurs, as one might expect, on the Seychelles Islands in the Indian Ocean. Apart from this species, the family comprises three large genera – *Hyperolius*, *Leptopelis* and *Afrixalus* – and ten small ones. The 106 species of *Hyperolius* are known as reed frogs or sedge frogs and are found ubiquitously throughout their range amongst the reedy margins of lakes, swamps and ponds, often in the centres of cities. All have expanded toe-pads and climb well and the males are characterised by their large vocal sacs, which dwarf the rest of their body when they are inflated. Several species show extreme variability in markings, even within the same population (see page 33), and this can make identification difficult. Southern African species all lay their eggs amongst submerged aquatic vegetation but some of the forms from West Africa attach their spawn to the stems of reeds, grasses, etc., and the tadpoles slide down into the water when they hatch. This is also the reproductive mode of all twenty-three species of *Afrixalus*, several of which also fold a leaf around their clutch – and are therefore known as leaf-folding frogs. *Afrixalus* differ from *Hyperolius* species in having vertical instead of horizontal pupils, and several species have small spiny tubercles on their skin, especially in males. *Leptopelis*, of which there are forty-one species, are not so arboreal as the previous two species and have plumper bodies and less well-developed toe-pads. Some species live in fairly arid situations and resort to burrowing to avoid desiccation. They spawn in burrows or depressions near to water and their tadpoles wriggle to water.

The genus *Kassina* contains the running frogs, e.g. *K. senegalensis* and *K. weali*, ground-dwelling species which are striped boldly in order to escape notice amongst the grasses in which they live, and the spotted *K. maculata*, a larger species which is primarily aquatic but also climbs well. The genus *Tornierella* contains two species from Ethiopia which were known as *Kassina* until recently. Both are medium-sized (up to 50 mm), terrestrial species which live beneath boulders, etc., and feed exclusively on slugs and snails. *Heterixalus* contains twelve species which are restricted to Madagascar, and the remaining eight genera contain one, two or three species each, often with restricted ranges in West or Central Africa; their natural history is not well known.

Rhacophoridae

The rhacophorids are mostly tree frogs, from Asia and Africa, where they fill the same niche as the *Hyla*, *Agalychnis* and *Phyllomedusa* species, etc., in the American tropics. Ten genera are recognised, seven from Asia, two from Madagascar and one, *Chiromantis*, from Africa. The latter are grey tree frogs, well known for their large arboreal foam nests and their ability (*C. xerampelina* and *C. petersi*) to withstand dry conditions (see page 41).

The fifty-six species of *Rhacophorus* are all highly arboreal species, living in the upper layers of rain forests from India and Japan to Indonesia. A number of species, of which the best known are *R. reinwardtii* and *R. nigropalmatus* (plate 12) have fringes and flaps to their limbs and enormous hands and feet which are extensively webbed and enable them to glide from high trees. Many of these species are brightly marked. Most species build arboreal foam nests, but the eggs of *R. kajua* from Borneo are laid as a single layer attached to a leaf overhanging water, and *R. harrissoni* breeds in holes in trees or between the buttresses of large forest trees.

Of the eleven species of *Polypedates*, *P. leucomystax* is by far the commonest, living in secondary forests, around villages and even within the

Plate 99   *Microhyla berdmorei* is a rain forest species from the Malaysian peninsular, where several similar species are found.

boundaries of large cities. The members of this genus also build foam nests and *P. leucomystax* often uses old concrete cisterns and metal water butts in which to breed. *Philautus* (sixty-three species) are inconspicuous arboreal frogs about which little appears to be known, although at least some species breed in tree-holes and have non-feeding tadpoles. Certain *Theloderma* and *Nyctixalus* species probably breed in the same way, are also inhabitants of dense rain forests, and are rarely seen.

Aglyptodactylus madagascariensis differs from the rest of the family in being terrestrial rather than arboreal, and both it and the twenty-eight other Madagascan species (genus *Boophis*) lay small eggs in water. The

178

Plate 100   *Gastrophryne olivacea*, the plains narrow-mouthed toad, is one of only two microhylid species found in North America.

remaining genera are *Buergia*, with four species from Taiwan to Japan, and *Chirixalus*, with four species in South East Asia. Members of both genera apparently build foam nests but are not well studied.

Microhylidae

The microhylids are a diverse group of 279 small to medium sized frogs living in many parts of the world, where they seem to fill the niches which other frogs can't reach. Many of them burrow or live amongst leaf-litter, but in Madagascar, where there are few arboreal frogs, several

179

have taken to the trees. Their distribution is interesting: their strong-holds seem to be New Guinea, where there are about ninety species, making up half of the frog population of that region, and Madagascar, where there are fifty species, but others are also found in South America, North America, Africa and Asia.

The New Guinea species are divided into twelve genera. Most species live on or under the forest floor, and these include the strange *Asterophrys turpicula*, which is large for a microhylid (up to 65 mm), has fleshy horns over its eyes and feeds on lizards as well as insects. Other species live amongst tussock grass at fairly high altitudes and several, especially the sixteen species of *Cophixalus* from the region, are arboreal and have expanded toe-pads. All microhylids in New Guinea and its surrounding islands lay terrestrial eggs which undergo direct development.

In Madagascar there are several terrestrial species such as *Dyscophus antongilii* which, owing to its shape and coloration, is known as the tomato frog, but most species seem to be arboreal. Many of these probably breed in tree-holes, e.g. *Platyhyla*, or leaf-axils, e.g. *Plethodontohyla*. The African *Breviceps* species are known as rain frogs. All twelve species are globular in shape with short heads and blunt snouts, and are exclusively burrowing frogs, some in arid regions, and others in forests, laying their eggs in underground chambers and producing non-feeding tadpoles. The four species of *Phrynomerus*, also from Africa, are sometimes known as rubber frogs – they are pear-shaped, smooth-skinned species which are black with red or pink markings. They breed in flood waters.

Most familiar of the South East Asian species is *Kaloula pulchra* (plate 76), the painted frog or bullfrog. It is only found in the vicinity of villages, city parks, etc., and has increased its range in many places by accompanying man on his travels. It calls with a cow-like moan after heavy rains and breeds in puddles and ditches. Other Asian species include those belonging to the genus *Microhyla* (plate 99), small agile species which breed in temporary pools, and *Kalophrynus*, forest species which produce non-feeding tadpoles.

In the New World two species of *Gastrophryne* (plate 100) range as far north as the United States, while in Central and South America about forty species are split into fifteen genera, many of which contain only one species and have strange names such as *Relictivomer*, *Stereocyclops* and *Dasypops*! As far as is known, all are burrowing species and are rarely seen, and all lay small eggs in water.

Many microhylids undoubtedly await discovery, as many are small, secretive and unspectacular in appearance, the areas in which they are found are little explored herpetologically, and they are notoriously diffi-cult to identify.

Bibliography

Biology of frogs and toads, and general accounts

Apart from a few notable books which deal with the biology of frogs in its entirety, much of the information is contained in numerous scientific journals, only a few of which can be listed here. A comprehensive list of references can be found in Duellman and Trueb (see below).

Channing, A. 1976. Life histories of frogs in the Namib Desert. *Zool. Africana*, 11:299–312.

Cochran, D. M. 1961. *Living Amphibians of the World*. Hamish Hamilton, London.

Coe, M. J., 1974. Observations of the ecology and breeding biology of the genus *Chiromantis*. *J. Zool. (London)*, 172:13–34.

Corben, C. J.; Ingram, G. J. and Tyler, M. J., 1974. Gastric brooding, a unique form of parental care in an Australian frog. *Science*, 186:946–947.

Crump, M. L., 1974. Reproductive strategies in a tropical anuran community. *Misc. Publ. Mus. Nat. Hist. Univ. Kansas*, 61:1–68.

Davies, N. B. and Halliday, T. R., 1977. Optimal mate selection in the toad *Bufo bufo*. *Nature*, 269, 56–58.

Duellman, W. E. and Maness, S. J., 1980. The reproductive behaviour of some hylid marsupial frogs. *J. Herpetol.*, 14:213–222.

Duellman, W. E. and Trueb, L., 1985. *Biology of Amphibians*. McGraw-Hill Book Company, New York. (The best book of its kind – essential reading.)

Goin, C. J., Goin, O. B. and Zug, G. R., 1978. *Introduction to Herpetology*, (third edition). W. H. Freeman and Company, San Francisco.

Koestler, A., 1971. *The Case of the Midwife Toad*. Hutchinson and Company, London. (Not really a biology book, but an interesting account of the scientist Paul Kammerer, and his work on evolution.)

McDiarmid, R. W., 1978. Evolution of parental care amongst frogs. In G. M. Burghardt and M. Bekoff (eds): *The Development of Behaviour: Comparative and Evolutionary Aspects*, pages 127–147. STPM Press, New York.

Porter, K. R., 1972. *Herpetology*. W. B. Saunders Company, Philadelphia.

Rabb, G. B. and Rabb, M. S., 1961. On the mating and egg-laying behaviour of the Surinam toad, *Pipa pipa*. *Copeia*, 1960:271–276.

Rabb, G. B. and Rabb, M. S., 1963. On the behaviour and breeding biology of the African pipid frog *Hymenochirus boettgeri*. *Zeit. Tierpschol.*, 20:215–241.

Roberts, J. D., 1984. Terrestrial egg deposition and direct development in *Arenophryne rotunda* Tyler: a myobatrachid frog from coastal sand dunes at Shark Bay, Western Australia. *Australian Wildl. Res.* 11:191–200.

Tuttle, M. D. and Ryan, M. J., 1981. Bat predation and the evolution of frog vocalisation in the tropics. *Science,* 214:677–678.

Tyler, M. J., 1976. *Frogs.* Collins Ltd., Sydney. (Australian Naturalists Library.) (Concerned mainly with Australasian species, but very readable.)

Wake, M. H., 1978. The reproductive biology of *Eleutherodactylus jasperi,* with comments on the evolution of live-bearing systems. *J. Herpetol.* 12:121–133.

Wake, M. H., 1980. The reproductive biology of *Nectophrynoides malcomi,* with comments on the evolution of reproductive modes in the genus *Nectophrynoides. Copeia* 1980:193–209.

Wells, K. D., 1977. The social behaviour of anuran amphibians. *Animal Behaviour,* 25:666–693.

Taxonomic revisions, etc.

Groups of frogs, and their names, are being revised constantly by scientists all over the world: much of this information is only of academic interest as far as the average naturalist is concerned, but some of these articles contain notes on the ecology, life-histories, etc., of the animals and make interesting reading. This list, which is far from complete, gives a small sample of papers which have a wider appeal than many of their titles would suggest.

Drewes, R. C., 1984. A phylogenetic analysis of the Hyperoliidae (Anura): treefrogs of Africa, Madagascar and the Seychelles Islands. *Occ. Pap. California Acad. Sci.,* 139:1–70.

Duellman, W. E., 1970. The hylid frogs of Middle America. *Monog. Mus. Nat. Hist. Univ. Kansas* 1:1–753. (A superb publication, well written and beautifully illustrated.)

Duellman, W. E., 1974. A systematic review of the marsupial frogs (Hylidae: *Gastrotheca*) of the Andes of Ecuador. *Occ. Pap. Mus. Nat. Hist., Univ. Kansas,* 22:1–27.

Duellman, W. E. and Fritts, T. H., 1972. A taxonomic review of the southern Andean marsupial frogs (Hylidae: *Gastrotheca*). *Occ. Pap. Mus. Nat. Hist., Univ. Kansas,* 9:1–37.

Lutz, B., 1973. *Brazilian species of Hyla.* Univ. Texas Press, Austin.

Lynch, J. D., 1971. Evolutionary relationships, osteology and zoogeography of leptodactylid frogs. *Misc. Publ. Mus. Nat. Hist. Univ. Kansas.,* 53:1–238. (Heavy-going but an important survey of a large and difficult group of frogs.)

Lynch, J. D. and Duellman, W. E., 1973. A review of the centrolenid frogs of Ecuador, with descriptions of new species. *Occ. Pap. Mus. Nat. Hist. Univ. Kansas.,* 16:1–66.

Myers, C. W. and Daly, J. W., 1983. Dart-poison frogs. *Sci. Amer.*, 248(2):120–133.

Myers, C. W., Daly, J. W. and Malkin, B., 1978. A dangerously toxic new frog (*Phyllobates*) used by the Embera Indians of Western Colombia, with discussion of blowgun fabrication and dart poisoning. *Bull. Amer. Mus. Nat. Hist.*, 161:307–366. (Fascinating reading.)

Peters, J. A., 1973. The frog genus *Atelopus* in Ecuador. *Smithsonian Contributions to Zoology*, 145:1–49.

Schiøtz, A., 1967. The treefrogs (Rhacophoridae) of West Africa. *Spol. Zool. Mus. Haun. (Copenhagen)*, 25:1–346. (This account also deals with the treefrogs now placed in the Hyperoliidae.)

Schiøtz, A., 1975. *The treefrogs of Eastern Africa*. Steenstrupia, Copenhagen.

Silverstone, P. A., 1975. A revision of the poison arrow frogs of the genus *Dendrobates* Wagler. *Nat. Hist. Mus. Los Angeles Co. Sci. Bull.*, 21:1–55.

Silverstone, P. A., 1976. A revision of the poison-arrow frogs of the genus *Phyllobates* Bibron. *Nat. Hist. Mus. Los Angeles Co. Sci. Bull.*, 27:1–53.

Trueb, L., 1971. Phylogenetic relationships of certain Neotropical toads with the description of a new genus (Anura: Bufonidae). *Nat. Hist. Mus. Los Angeles Co. Contributions in Science*, 216:1–40 (An account of the genus *Rhamphophryne*.)

Trueb, L., 1974. Systematic relationships of Neotropical horned frogs, genus *Hemiphractus* (Anura: Hylidae). *Occ. Pap. Mus. Nat. Hist. Univ. Kansas*, 29:1–60.

Trueb, L. and Tyler, M. J., 1974. Systematics and evolution of the Greater Antillean hylid frogs. *Occ. Pap. Mus. Nat. Hist. Univ. Kansas*, 24:1–60.

Tyler, M. J., 1963a. A taxonomic study of the amphibians and reptiles of the central highlands of New Guinea, with notes of their ecology and biology. I. Anura: Microhylidae. *Trans. Roy. Soc. S. Australia*, 86:11–29.

Tyler, M. J., 1963b. A taxonomic study of the amphibians and reptiles of the central highlands of New Guinea, with notes on their ecology and biology. II. Anura: Ranidae and Hylidae. *Trans. Roy. Soc. S. Australia*, 86:105–130.

Field Guides and Keys

Listed here are publications which may be useful in the identification of frogs and toads. Some are highly scientific but most are fairly easy to follow. Those which are asterisked provide illustrations of all or most of the species with which they deal. Most keys are to the adult form but a few also provide the means of identifying, at least to genus, tadpoles. Unfortunately, many of these publications are now out of print but may be obtainable through secondhand dealers, public or university libraries. As usual, some areas are far better covered than others.

Altig, R., 1970. A key to the tadpoles of continental United States and Canada. *Herpetologica*, 26:180–207.

**Arnold, E. N. and Burton, J. A., 1978. *A Field Guide to the Reptiles and Amphibians of Britain and Europe*. Collins, London.

*Berry, P. Y., 1975. *The Amphibian Fauna of Peninsular Malaysia*. Tropical Press, Kuala Lumpur.

Cei, J. M., 1962. *Batrachios de Chile*. Univ. Chile, Santiago.

**Cei, J. M., 1980. Amphibians of Argentina. *Monit. Zool. Italiano N. S. Monog.*, 2:1–609.

Cochran, D. M., 1955. Frogs of Southeastern Brazil. *Bull. U. S. Natl. Mus.*, 206:1–423.

Cochran, D. M., 1970. Frogs of Colombia. *Bull. U. S. Natl. Mus.*, 288:1–655.

**Cogger, H. G., 1979. *Reptiles and Amphibians of Australia*, rev. ed. A. H. and A. W. Reed Pty Ltd, Sydney.

**Conant, R., 1969. *A Field Guide to Reptiles and Amphibians of Eastern North America*, rev. ed. Houghton Mifflin Co., Boston.

*Duellman, W. E., 1978. The biology of an equatorial herpetofauna in Amazonian Ecuador. *Misc. Publ. Mus. Nat. Hist. Univ. Kansas*, 65:1–352.

*Frazer, D., 1983. *Reptiles and Amphibians in Britain*. Collins, London.

*Henderson, R. W. and Schwartz, A., 1984. *A Guide to the Reptiles and Amphibians of Hispaniola*. Milwaukee Public Museum, Milwaukee.

Inger, R. F., 1954. Systematics and zoogeography of Philippine Amphibia. *Fieldiana Zool.*, 33:181–531.

Inger, R. F., 1966. The systematics and zoogeography of the Amphibia of Borneo. *Fieldiana Zool.*, 52:1–402.

Inger, R. F., 1985. Tadpoles of the forested regions of Borneo. *Fieldiana Zool.*, new series, 26:1–89.

Inger, R. F., Voris, H. K. and Walker, P., 1985. A key to the frogs of Sarawak. *Sarawak Mus. Journal*, new series, 55:161–182.

Kenny, J. S., 1969. The Amphibia of Trinidad. *Stud. Fauna Curacao Caribbean Isl.*, 29:1–78.

**McKeown, S., 1978. *Hawaiian Reptiles and Amphibians*. Oriental Publishing Company, Honolulu.

**Menzies, J. I., 1976. *Handbook of Common New Guinea Frogs*. Wau Ecology Institute, Handbook no. 1.

Meyer, J. R. and Wilson, L. D., 1971. A distributional checklist of the amphibians of Honduras. *Nat. Hist. Mus. Los Angeles Co. Contr. Sci.*, 218:1–47.

**Passmore, N. I. and Carruthers, V. C., 1979. *South African Frogs*. Witwatersrand Univ. Press, Johannesburg.

*Poynton, J. C., 1964. The amphibia of southern Africa. *Ann. Natal Mus.*, 17:1–334.

**Rivero, J. A., 1978. *Los Anfibios y reptiles de Puerto Rico*. Educ. Universidad Puerto Rico, San Juan. (In Spanish and English.)

**Robb, J., 1980. *New Zealand Reptiles and Amphibians in Colour*. Collins, Auckland.

**Schwartz, A. and Henderson, R. W., 1975. *A Guide to the Identification of* *the Amphibians and Reptiles of the West Indies, exclusive of Hispaniola.* Milwaukee Public Museum, Milwaukee.

**Stebbins, R. C., 1966. *A Field Guide to Western Reptiles and Amphibians.* Houghton Mifflin Co., Boston.

Taylor, E. H., 1962. The amphibian fauna of Thailand. *Univ. Kansas Sci. Bull.*, 36:265–599.

Tyler, M. J., 1977. *Frogs of South Australia.* South Australian Museum, Adelaide.

**Tyler, M. J., Smith, L. A. and Johnstone, R. E., 1984. *Frogs of Western Australia.* Western Australian Museum, Perth.

*Wright, A. H. and Wright, A. A., 1949. *Handbook of Frogs and Toads of the United States and Canada.* Comstock Publishing Co., Ithaca.

Zweifel, R. G. and Tyler, M. J., 1982. Amphibia of New Guinea. *Monographiae Biologicae*, 42:759–801.

* Indicates that a substantial number of the species are illustrated in black and white.
** Indicates that a substantial number of the species are illustrated in colour, although there may also be some species illustrated in black and white.
The other publications may contain photographs of some species only or they may be lacking illustrations altogether.

Recordings

The wide diversity of calls produced by male frogs of different species provides ample scope for sound recordists. To the best of my knowledge, only three such recordings are commercially available, but hopefully it will not be too long before this list is extended.

Bogert, C. M. Sounds of North American Frogs: the Biological Significance of Voice in Frogs. Folkway Records, New York. (12 in LP disc with 92 calls of 50 species of North American species, with accompanying text.)

Kellogg, P. P. and Allen, A. A. Voices of the Night. Houghton Mifflin and Cornell Laboratory of Ornithology. (12 in LP disc with the calls of 34 species of eastern North American frogs and toads.)

Passmore, N. I. and Carruthers, V. C. Voices of South African Frogs. Witwatersrand University Press, Johannesburg. (7 in disc with the calls of 74 species of frogs and toads – a companion to the book by the same authors.)

Index

In order to avoid repetition throughout the book, common names are often used only once, with latinised names being used thereafter. Since this index has been compiled according to actual references in the book, the common name of a species may have only one or two entries whereas its latinised name has several. It is possible, however, to find all of the relevant passages, even if only the common name is known, by cross-reference.

Figures in **bold** refer to page numbers of illustrations.